Running to Resurrection

'Reading *Running to Resurrection* reminded me of the words of St Irenaeus of Lyons: "The glory of God is a human being fully alive". This book is about Brother Clark Berge SSF's journey to becoming a whole human being. Particularly in relation to being an alcoholic, it is a profoundly inspiring story of redemption. While being deeply challenged and healthily disturbed, I loved the way Clark integrated the relationship between our physical bodies and our spiritual journeys, making reference to a wide range of texts to illuminate what he says. His deep honesty about his own brokenness and innermost struggles, and his degree of self-disclosure and vulnerability, will encourage many on their own tortuous journeys towards resurrection. While the book will have particular resonance for members of religious orders, those suffering from addictions and same-gender-loving persons, all of us on our own journeys of discipleship will be encouraged by what they read. Using his time as Minister General of the Franciscans living in greatly varied contexts, interwoven with running as the backdrop to much of the book, enables the reader to also harvest the fruit of those years. The ability of Brother Clark to describe places and the continuum of the physical, sexual, emotional and spiritual gives the writing a visceral quality. While the book has many memorable passages, I especially loved his homily to the baboons. *Running to Resurrection* is food for the soul and invites all of us to participate in the resurrection here and now. I am sure St Francis of Assisi enjoyed reading it as much as I did and you will too'. *Father Michael Lapsley SSM, Institute for Healing of Memories, Cape Town, South Africa*

Also by Clark Berge

The Vows Book: Anglican Teaching on the Vows of Obedience, Poverty and Chastity
CreateSpace Independent Publishing Platform

For Elizabeth,
Peace and all
good!

Running to Resurrection

A Soul-making Chronicle

Clark Berge

With every
best wish,

Clark Berge

CANTERBURY
PRESS

Norwich

First published in 2019 by the Canterbury Press Norwich
Editorial office
3rd Floor, Invicta House
108–114 Golden Lane
London EC1Y 0TG, UK
www.canterburypress.co.uk

Canterbury Press is an imprint of Hymns Ancient & Modern Ltd
(a registered charity)

Hymns Ancient & Modern® is a registered trademark of
Hymns Ancient & Modern Ltd
13A Hellesdon Park Road, Norwich,
Norfolk NR6 5DR, UK

Scripture quotations are from the New Revised Standard Version of the
Bible, Anglicized Edition, copyright © 1989, 1995 by the Division of Christian
Education of the National Council of the Churches of Christ in the USA. Used by
permission. All rights reserved.

British Library Cataloguing in Publication data

A catalogue record for this book is available
from the British Library

978 1 78622 216 9

Printed and bound in Great Britain by CPI Group (UK) Ltd

With love and gratitude to my mother,
Marian Berge

I appeal to you therefore, brothers and sisters, by the mercies of God, to present your bodies as a living sacrifice, holy and acceptable to God, which is your spiritual worship. Do not be conformed to this world, but be transformed by the renewing of your minds, so that you may discern what is the will of God – what is good and acceptable and perfect.

Romans 12.1-2

Contents

Acknowledgements

First, thanks to my family, my mother and late father, my siblings and their families whose love and support is unconditional.

Thanks to my brothers in the Society of St Francis around the world for their help and support. It has been an adventure growing up in our community. The stories I tell about our life together are told with deep affection. It was an honour to be the Minister General and I am grateful every day for our Franciscan vocation.

I also wish to thank the community of recovering alcoholics around the world who have listened, laughed and cried with me, and pushed me to reflect deeply on my life and to change the way I think and live. Because of them I have had a taste of a life that is happy, joyous and free.

For intellectual stimulation and inspiration during long walks in San Francisco, thanks to Dave Richo. Paula Gooder's book *Body* had an electrifying, liberating impact on me. The book provided a biblical and theological grounding for my reflections, giving them some *gravitas*. I feel that the way she presents St Paul in a new light is a huge gift to Christians, especially those wishing to heal wounding ideas about their bodies. Although I have never met her, I feel a kinship with her and am grateful for her work. I owe so much to the late Jon Bankert SSF for his loving, provocative friendship, helping me to discover the joys and pains of religious life and to persevere in our vocation.

In preparing this typescript for publication many thanks to VK McCarty for flying to England and spending a week poring over the penultimate draft of this book, sharing her prodigious skill and devotion in editing. She is a dear friend. Thanks to Lorena Touchet, Andy Quinn, Richard Carter, Patrick Woodhouse and my mother for reading and commenting on the typescript with care and insight. Thanks to Patrick Woodhouse for his beautiful photograph of me, and to him and his wife Sam for their great encouragement in all things.

My gratitude goes to Linda Carroll and Joanne Hill and also to Christine Smith, Mary Matthews, Rachel Geddes, Josie Gunn and all at Canterbury Press for their advice, support and hard work.

And a great shout out to the universe for the joy of running, experiencing the presence and love of God in so many places, with so many people, on such a beautiful, fragile earth.

Introduction

Soul-making ... includes our bodies ... Intentional soul-making involves paying attention to movements, activities and relationships that animate us and seeking to engage in something that brings life to as many aspects of our being as possible, as regularly as possible. (Paula Gooder, *Body*, p. 42)

Running has become a wide-open frontier where my body and spirituality converge, a playground of embodied living. I realized this when a friend asked me about my running during our weekly Bible study.

When I run, I told her, I feel joy in the beauty of the plants and trees, the seashore, the animals and birds I see. I feel part of the neighbourhood, and love greeting people. I feel refreshed even when I am physically tired. I feel stronger, more light-hearted. Often, I solve problems that are preoccupying me, if only to decide they aren't really problems. I can even shake off writer's block in sermon preparation.

Molly looked at me for a moment, then commented: 'That sounds like prayer.'

Exploring this prayerful, playful practice is the story of this book. Running has helped heal some wounds I've suffered for a long time, it has forced me to reckon with my strengths and weaknesses, gifts and liabilities as an adult. Running has opened a path for me to what Eugene Peterson in *Practice Resurrection* calls 'resurrection life'. For years I'd lived with the 'blahs', a dull, half-asleep feeling. Like a rainy Saturday afternoon, this feeling hung between me and the world, blocking the sun, thwarting the unfettered joy for which I longed. There wasn't a crisis, but after five years without alcohol and nearly 15 years as a Franciscan brother I had to acknowledge that something still wasn't right with my life. The heaviness of my heart and belly weighed on me. Eventually, just living with that feeling wasn't good enough. I had no idea what the cause of my problems was. Physically, I was very aware of, and impatient with, lower back pain. Emotionally, I still felt a festering irritation with life and lashed out at others with angry words and gestures, though I worked on changing these behaviours with a therapist and in recovery from alcoholism. My spiritual life was more by rote than a real adventure. And I was only 45 years old. I began to explore different kinds of healing.

A chiropractor kneading my spine and coccyx planted the first disquieting seed of a conversion to a more active life by asking what kind of exercise I did. 'Clean the house, rake the grass, wash windows,' I reeled off the list defensively, in the same manner I'd snap before when people asked how much I drank: 'Not that much!' Whoever said half a case of beer was too much? Deep down, after five years without drinking, I knew he was looking for a different answer. I repented of my sarcasm but was reluctant to put in more effort to feel better. Wasn't that his job?

In this badgered frame of mind and body I went on retreat, taking with me a book by Matthew Fox, *Sins of the Spirit, Blessings of the Flesh*. On the second day of my retreat, I flopped lazily on my bed and began thumbing through Fox's book. I ate some chocolate chip cookies.

In his book, Fox begins by writing about the blessings of the flesh, with wide-ranging insights from spirituality, science and art. A review of sin and its various meanings leads into a section on the sins of the spirit. Finally, he goes through the seven *chakras* (the classic energy centres in the body, important to Eastern spirituality), correlating them with the seven capital sins. It was his description of the sins of the Spirit related to the first chakra at the base of the spine – that chiropractor had his finger on it – that rocked my world.

Challenging the sin of 'couch potato-itis' as one of the daughters of *acedia* (meaning listless torpor, apathy), a symptom of an unawakened first chakra, Fox writes: 'Acedia is the first of the sins of the spirit because it is where our energy dries up. The lesson learned here is that *a life without cosmology and a life without relationships is an energy-less life*' (p. 170). I wasn't lazy, but charging through my chores resentfully wasn't exactly a life of joy and fulfilment. It was like being emotionally constipated. I needed to awaken my first chakra.

Contrasted to this lacklustre existence, Fox quotes Bill McKibben, author, educator, environmentalist and co-founder of 350.org, recalling the simple activity of swimming, which can include a real cosmological connection to the environment and a sense of joy, things that need to be incorporated into our lives:

> I can feel water rushing past my head, smoothing back my hair ... I haul myself out onto a rock in the middle of the pond and sit there dripping. A breeze comes up, and lifts the hairs on my back, each one giving a nearly imperceptible tug at my skin. Under hand and thigh, I can feel the roughness and the hardness of the rock. If I listen, I can hear the birds singing from several trees around the shore, and a frog now and again ... I can see a hundred things – the sun reflects off the ripples ... I can smell the water. (McKibben, *The Age of Missing Information*, quoted in Fox, *Sins of the Spirit*, p. 102)

I felt my heart leap at the description of the pond swim and remembered roughhousing with my brother in the Snoqualmie river during childhood summers. What happened to me?

For Fox, life in the Spirit means waking up. He quotes the poet Rumi:

The way you distinguish a true commentary from a false is this: Whichever explication makes you feel fiery and hopeful, humble and active, that's the true one. If it makes you lazy, it's not right. (Fox, *Sins of the Spirit*, p. 118)

Since then I have found other theologians corroborating these easily overlooked insights. In her book *Body: Biblical Spirituality for the Whole Person*, Paula Gooder exegetes some of the bedevilling complexities of St Paul's writing in a fiery, hopeful way, explaining Paul's thought in a completely body-positive light. In the popular Christian imagination, his writings have had a far-reaching impact, much of it negative, about the body. Summarizing her biblical study of St Paul, Gooder writes:

> Our bodies are an integral part of Spirituality in that what we do with our bodies should live up to the knowledge that they are the temple of God's Spirit. If we do not look after our bodies – if we allow them to become worn out and crumbling temples for God's Spirit – then we do not cherish the great privilege that God has given us. An embodied Spirituality requires us to recognize not only that what we do with and to our bodies must live up to our calling to be worthy temples of God's Spirit in the world, but also that God's Spirit, by its very nature, brings life. If we abuse our bodies in any way (by overworking, not resting enough, ignoring what our bodies tell us about our well-being) then we are not allowing the Spirit to work fully within us. Taking proper care of our bodies – those temples of the Holy Spirit – should be ranked alongside prayer as a Spiritual discipline. (Gooder, *Body*, p. 86)

What was I doing? I was addressing my spiritual and physical needs superficially. I was self-medicating with too much food and too much work to assuage the absence of alcohol. I hardly gave my prayer life a chance, the daily round of prayer services huffed through impatiently and punctiliously. Perhaps the tiredness and impatience in my life was a symptom of a deeper disease: a desire

4

for a connection with God that involved all of me, not just my overworked brain.

Could it be, too, that the back pain and low-grade depression were as much as anything else a cry from my body for help? I had ignored my body for a long time. I'd talked about the spiritual life for 20 years and, as I mulled over Fox's words, recumbent in my chocolate-flecked bed, I felt an uneasy awareness such as I feel when I realize I haven't been completely honest with myself or another person. I recognized his description of acedia, as if he'd been following me around. The thrust of his book was that true spirituality is never just an intellectual proposition, but a lived, embodied, reality. I had a fidgety sense that I needed to get up and move, joyfully and vigorously, not just take on more work. Most of the year, pond swimming, or any kind of swimming alfresco, was out of the question. But everything McKibben described, I wanted.

It wasn't a sudden epiphany but a gradual sense of a commitment that coalesced that day on retreat. I needed to change my life. I started to toy with the idea of jogging, the only exercise I could imagine doing. Attracted by Fox's argument for integration, I set out for my first run. The desire to feel better trumped my shame for a moment. And that was long enough to get me out of the door in a pair of canvas shoes, Bermuda shorts and a short-sleeve shirt. Hardly running gear, but they were the only clothes I had for this impromptu sprint up the steep driveway away from the monastery. Some 100 yards along, my breath was ragged with phlegm. I was puffing like a pair of bellows. My calves hurt, and I was so self-conscious I turned back, praying nobody had seen me. But in the days ahead I persisted. My dream for myself was that I could be the kind of person who lives a vigorous, physical, happy life.

Challenging the belief in me that I didn't need exercise seemed to take ages. The layers of fear, anger and shame had immobilized me athletically for years. My disquiet got worse as I imagined the mocking and derogatory comments of others observing me pursuing some kind of sport or exercise regime. I am not the only gay kid to have suffered taunts and ridicule in physical education, and probably not the first to vow to never expose myself to such humiliation ever again. As a young adult whenever I felt awkward and insecure I would become defensive and dismissive of others. I often lashed out with belittling comments and judged others harshly, rarely making the effort to get to know them. Jocks were dumb and brutish – and beautiful and desirable, which made me afraid of them. Pre-judging or prejudice diminished my world into a safe little closet. My beliefs about exercise had served to protect me from the things I feared, like being ridiculed. Even subsequently as an adult I used words to describe my running like 'lumbering' and 'galumphing' that betrayed my ongoing anxiety about what I was doing. My recurring story was that I was uncoordinated, slow. Consequently, this made me useless, no good, and a loser. With a story like that who needs enemies?

It was saddening to realize that the only derogatory comments made about my physical prowess or athletic abilities since I was 14 were offered by myself. I'd linked every scathing remark from my adolescent peers into a litany I chanted whenever I felt exposed and vulnerable. I cudgelled myself with these frustrated jibes. Consequently, I'd told myself I did not need exercise, I was above all of that. I built a wall between me and anything that I considered athletic, quoting the cartoonist Paul Terry who famously said in 1937: 'Whenever I get the urge to exercise, I lie down until the feeling passes away.'[1] I had to change my accustomed thought patterns if I wanted a different kind of life.

The new story I had to tell myself as a runner was simple. Coached by a persistent therapist and diligent reading of self-help books, I worked to cut out the cynical humour and negative value judgements. I was not good at sports when I was a boy. I feel anger and grief that I missed out on an important part of growing up. I was hurt by the teasing of my contemporaries, but I can forgive them. And while I can't go back and change my past, I can develop ways to be physically active (Richo, *Daring to Trust*, pp. 94–5).

Every few days I donned my running gear and ran a short distance at a measured pace, feeling a bit foolish, a bit daring, and determined to keep my efforts at running a kind of play time. I knew well enough that deciding to train at the outset for a marathon or setting other grandiose goals would leach the joy from these initial efforts. No chance I'd stick with a misery-inducing discipline. I'd brought enough misery into my life and was determined to do things differently. For months, I jogged just a mile. Then one day I did 2 miles and felt like Hermes, the messenger of Olympus, quick as a flash, the ancient god of athletes. Gradually over a year's time I worked up to 6 miles on one sultry June morning. It was exhilarating!

There were measurable physical changes, too. I recovered my waist, I no longer had back pain. I rediscovered joy in my prayer life. I felt better in every way.

The experiences of running and the counsels of sobriety have been, and continue to be, absorbed slowly into my frontal lobes through the thick armour of pride, impatience and ignorance of myself. In early sobriety, I felt attacked by random-seeming pieces of advice: 'Watch it!' 'Cool down!' 'How'd you feel if somebody said that to you?' I'd go to my room to lick my wounds, mimicking my advisers sarcastically, lost in a self-pitying funk. But I could not defend myself completely from their common sense, because I'd publicly declared myself willing to do whatever it took to change my default character settings. Getting out of my room and jogging along the road felt like a prison breakout. Alone on the road I discovered I could pull the comments from the wallet of my memory and reconsider them. The solitude of the road became the sounding board of my conscience.

Solitude is different from loneliness or a vacuum devoid of joy and comforts – that is a hangover. Rather, it is an interior space I can access anywhere, even on a train or in a crowded room if need be. In my mental solitude, I find the space and privacy needed for my rebellious mind to thrash about to exhaustion, to give up futile resistance. Then my conscience, guided by God, slices deep into my memory and emotions, cutting back the fatty tissues of excuses, denials and fear. Then spiritual balm gets smeared on the raw places with remembered words of Scripture or a beautiful sight outdoors that draws me out of myself.

After all, Jesus sought solitude in wilderness locales. St Francis did too, going often to Mount Subasio and Mount La Verna to pray in caves and among the trees. Some people go into a room and close the door. Prospecting for the best approach to solitude is an essential piece of work for religious. I don't think I could have muscled my way much further in my vocation without learning that priority. I especially enjoy solitude when I'm suited up and hour after hour rhythmically pounding a road, following the crumbling edge of asphalt or a well-worn track. I've experienced the blessings of this solitude many times. Of course, sometimes I prefer getting lost in fantasies. But when I come to my senses, I feel I have squandered a fortune. 'Speak, Lord. Speak to me. I'm listening.'

In the 14 years since I began running, ten of those years I travelled around the world sharing life with my Franciscan brothers as a leader of the Episcopal/Anglican Society of St Francis. Franciscans are men and women who follow the example of St Francis of Assisi, a thirteenth-century saint who lived in modern-day Italy. The radical innovation of Francis for religious life of his time, along with Dominic, the founder of the Dominicans – the Order of Preachers – was that one could live a consecrated religious life outside the walls of a monastery. Francis founded an order of men who went about begging for alms, preaching and offering care and comfort wherever possible. Following the example of Francis, initially the brothers had a special care for lepers. Today, though we don't panhandle, we live very simply. Friars and sisters work with the poor and marginalized. We may serve in a parish or university, but our pastoral instincts are to support the outcast, the people on the edge. We take vows of obedience, poverty and chastity; for First Order brothers and sisters, and Second Order sisters, chastity means celibacy. Third Order members promise chastity, meaning fidelity to their spouse or partner. The designations of First, Second and Third notwithstanding, they are not hierarchical. First is not more important than Third. I always correlate them with the order in which Francis established them.

In 1937 our Anglican Order was founded, drawing together several small Francis-inspired groups that already existed. The much older American Congregation of the Poor Brethren of St Francis of Assisi joined up with the Society of St Francis based in the UK in 1966.

Each part of the Anglican Franciscan family has its own leader, a Minister General for First Order brothers, another Minister General for the First Order sisters, and yet another for the Third Order. The Second Order elects an Abbess. These four people serve as symbols of unity. To my astonishment, in 2007 I was elected Minister General of the First Order brothers. I am the first American to hold the office of Minister General. I felt the best way to serve the 140 brothers in the Order was to share their life in the disparate circumstances in which they live. I travelled year-round among five Franciscan provinces. The Order includes nine different countries and 24 friaries or households. I visited most of the same places year after year. Also, there were many invitations to visit other Anglican religious orders and to take part in ecumenical and interfaith occasions around the world. Although I met the Pope, the Ecumenical Patriarch, the Queen and a Fon from Cameroon, my heart was in the daily life of the brothers. Our regular round of prayer, community life and local ministry is the foundation of our witness. When these are happy and working well, our witness is powerful. Wherever I went I met with the brothers, got to know them and their circumstances, offered encouragement to them, and then took new insights from province to province. It was a cross-pollinating, itinerant ministry.

In every place I found running routes and pursued my athletic discipline *cum* body prayer. Every location with its culture and environment evoked nuances that contribute to the various insights of this book. Along the way, I learned to dispel with growing dexterity the shrapnel sprays of indiscriminate anger and recidivist self-hate that I tend to fling up at myself. My body is strong enough to withstand long flights, time changes, hard sleeping mats and lumpy mattresses, and a slew of different foods from familiar dishes to the really outré, such as whale blubber or possum.

Running along the roads of the world I have discovered what I needed to say when I needed to say it. And, occasionally, when to hold my peace, the sober restraint that makes so much difference in life.

St Augustine taught the concept of *solvitur ambulando* – it is solved by walking. It is only a small step further to rely on the benefits of jogging. It has become a way of participating in a larger grace-filled communal life that feels blessed, whole. In his book *Practice Resurrection*, Eugene Peterson notes:

'Practice Resurrection,' a phrase I got from Wendell Berry, strikes just the right note. We live our lives in the practice of what we do not originate and cannot anticipate. When we practice resurrection, we continuously enter into what is more than we are. When we practice resurrection, we keep company with Jesus, alive and present, who knows where we are going better than we do, which is always 'from glory unto glory' (p. 8).

That is my goal, I'm running to resurrection.

I'd be an unfaithful friar if I didn't share the treasure I've discovered. Jesus pointed out the signs of God's reign in the Gospels, I have been blessed with a few glimpses of my own. I hope this book leads you in some small way to discover your own ways of praying, to find healing for your physical and emotional stresses, to listen with an open mind to the needs of earth and human society, and to see and celebrate God at work in yourself, and the world around us. It's not so much that you should run, but that you should take your body seriously, develop a spiritual practice and remember that the stories we tell ourselves, the ideas we harbour, can either confine or liberate us. Be free.

Note

1 Printed in a syndicated gossip column based in New York on 13 June 1937. Available at: http://quoteinvestigator.com/2012/06/09/urge-to-exercise/ (accessed 9.12.16).

1

Creating a space for prayer: Mount Sinai, New York

Soul-making implies a deliberate intention on our part to pay attention to who we are called to be and to seek regular refreshment so that we can grow more and more into the people God yearns for us to be. (Gooder, *Body*, p. 42)

The proof of a pudding is in the tasting of it. The test of a New Year's resolution or a spiritual resolve after a retreat is usually whatever happens the week after. The flush of fervour wanes in the crush of obligations and distractions. It required gritting my teeth a bit, returning home after that inertia-breaking, body-animating spiritual retreat, but I kept up the momentum. Realizing I have always found time to do the things I really wanted to do, I gave myself an hour three times a week to run. I took the running in easy stages, and sought out the easiest, flattest route possible, gauging the grade of the hills and traffic patterns on local roads. Although the friary was built on a hilltop, it was close to the harbour and sea-level perimeter roads. The turn from the friary driveway was down a steep hill to the harbour, and the gravity seduced me, beckoning me to let go and run along the tree-shaded lanes.

Although I had visited the friary before I joined the Order, prior to taking up running my strongest memory of the roads around Little Portion friary - named after the birthplace of the Franciscan movement in Assisi - was when I arrived to test my vocation one day in October 1989. A friend had volunteered to drive me to the friary from New York City. As we approached Mount Sinai, the gut-roiling, nerve-wracking, hand-trembling implications of what I was doing crashed over me. Yelping to my friend to stop, I bailed out of the car as it was still rolling to vomit my lunch. 'Let's go back,' I said, 'I can't do this.'

'You've been thinking about this for a long time,' he reminded me. 'At least spend one night. I'll come back and get you, if you want.' We continued downhill along Mount Sinai-Coram Road. I had a warm reception from the six brothers who lived at Little Portion and decided to stay.

The brothers ran a guest house and gave retreats. Often one or two would be away visiting a parish to teach spirituality and to preach. To my joy there was a small bakery in the friary with ovens that got fired up every Friday morning, the brothers producing about 90 loaves. I had been baking bread since I was 11 and was very happy to plunge my hands into the dough. Over the weekend neighbours would come and buy the bread. From time to time we took a load of bread to local parish events to sell and to promote our life and ministry. During those first two years in the Order I baked bread, raised honey bees, planted a vegetable garden, and preached from time to time. I was only 30; it was a time of great blessings.

Some 60 miles east of Manhattan on the north shore of Long Island, in 1989 the village of Mount Sinai still retained some of its rural character. Peach farms, clam beds and winding tree-shaded roads surrounded the friary. The area was originally called Nonowantuk, purchased in 1664 from Sachem Massatewse, chief of the Setauket tribe. The English settlement was then called Old Man's (Becker, *Images of America*, p. 7), and for years there was the Old Man's boat yard at the crossroads of Old Post Road and Shore Road.

In 2004, after living in other friaries, and learning a few home-truths about my 'innocent' drinking, I started to search out a new way forward along these old roads. This route is my running 'womb'. I jog slowly down acorn-strewn roads shaded by oak, beech, black walnut and other hardwood trees. The deciduous woods are enlivened in winter with the darkly gleaming presence of holly trees and evergreen mountain laurel. In summer the dreamy drifts of flowering dogwood and black locust are like a ballet stage set, cooing doves providing a romantic soundtrack. Daredevil grey squirrels leap from branch to branch, making their way through the woodlands high above the ground. Groundhogs prowl hungrily around the vegetable garden's electric fence, deer prance showily across lawns and twilight roads. I run through a scene alive with elegant swans dallying among the reeds, horseshoe crabs doing whatever they do in the sandy shallows. Along a straight stretch bordering the shore I can see people digging clams from the pungent, boot-sucking mud. Beyond them I see friends' lobster boats moored in the deepest parts of the tidal harbour. Not only am I conscious of the beauty, but over time I have learned the backstory of many of the places I regularly pass. As the road swings up from the shore on a long gentle incline, I jog by a house Marilyn Monroe is reputed to have visited.

Getting out and running down the road isn't always pleasant either: I have memories of near misses with cars, slogging through the wind and rain. I recall moments of utter wretchedness, too – vomiting in the milkweed after a heavy Mexican lunch, unavoidable bowel movements under roadside shrubbery after my sphincter sent out a trickle of trembling emissaries signalling imminent collapse of my control. For better or worse, I am part of my surroundings – one of those scantily clad running people you see everywhere in the world.

But taking the exigencies of life in my stride has been a big part of my learning in sobriety. The larger picture is that being part of the landscape – not just talking about the environment or looking at it, but scuffing my feet in the dirt – is a way of praising God. The grateful consciousness of beauty is adoration. Alone on the road I have shouted out to the trees, hollered for sheer joy when I saw the sun on the waves. I have filled my lungs with the air summer and winter, snorting pollen and snowflakes. Running through nature, experiencing all the different weathers, interacting with people, motorists and animals I begin to grasp the idea that I dwell in God and God in me. I know in some ways I am puny and vulnerable – in other ways I have power. I am brought back to a grateful awareness of a huge world where I'm not in charge.

Running is a salutary reminder of whose world I inhabit.

Reaching a point when I have to stop running and walk for a while, I pick up litter to cover my inability to run, and to 'give back' to the beautiful neighbourhood. I collect armloads of beer cans, vodka bottles, empty cigarette packets, the occasional squishy condom and a tiny grudge against the littering bastards – all of which, grudge and all, I deposit in the nearest dumpster. Learning to pray with all this raw material is perhaps a Franciscan preoccupation. Prayer is the way I bring together the discipline of recovery and the discipline of running into my religious life. The rhythmic breathing of the exercise fits well with certain prayers. 'Say the Serenity Prayer,' I remind myself. I recite it like a mantra: 'God grant me the serenity to accept the things I cannot change, the courage to change the things I can, and the wisdom to know the difference.' When I finish, I'll say it again. Over and over again I pray the simple prayer until I can hold on to my core self. It's like all meditation practices: we keep coming back to a focus like the breath, or a simple prayer, letting go of distractions and disturbances. Sometimes it seems as if that is the reality of meditation – not extended periods of bliss, but repeated letting go as often as necessary, coming back to mindfulness, perhaps 70 times seven.

This repetition has helped me practise what I learned from reading Henri Nouwen's *Genesee Diary*, the discipline of *nepsis* or mental sobriety, the work to keep 'bad thoughts away and creating free space for prayer'. Reflecting on the fact that I cannot change other people, but I can change myself by practising acceptance and generosity towards myself and others, I can let go of the negative worries and preoccupations of friary life as I run along and enjoy times of prayer, following my breath, the rhythm of my feet.

Negative thinking starts innocently enough, like picking at mosquito bites. I begin to think about a hurt or a problem, or a relationship difficulty. Then, like a chemical reaction, it builds up to a boiling head of indignation and frustration. When this happens, and I am running, I sometimes find myself sprinting. But soon exhausted and brought up short, gasping for breath, I hear myself saying: 'I can't do this!' I can't sprint 6 miles, nor can I hold the peevish indignation and hurt. At that moment, there is a shift, what is called in Biospirituality[1] a bodily felt experience of grace. After I got sober, I picked up a line from a motivational speaker, which I think he got from Freud: 'Your body never lies!' When I am feeling angry or sad, there is often a physical symptom – a tight jaw, a squirming stomach. Yet my brain throws a body block and I lie about my feelings. 'I'm fine,' I say if anybody asks. In recovery, friends snort at this response, usually pointing out 'FINE' is an acronym: 'Fucked up, Insecure, Neurotic and Emotional'. Fine, indeed. Obviously, denying what my body is telling me doesn't make the anger or grief or hurt go away. Running has helped clear my mind and helps as well to name my feelings. By paying attention to the feeling and praying with it in a spirit of compassion, it changes. Sometimes the feelings go away, sometimes they feed a deeper sense of God's activity in my life.

I've learned to take my feelings seriously as clues to deeper self-knowledge. Eugene Gendlin, the founder of the Focusing movement, teaches: 'Your physically felt body is in fact part of a gigantic system of here and other places, you and other people – in fact the whole universe. This sense of being bodily alive in a vast system is the body as it's felt from the inside.' (Gendlin, *Focusing*, cited in Richo, *When the Past is Present*, p. 123). Being aware of my part in the universe gives me a sense of power. I have power to pay attention to my feelings, as well as to move, to breathe, pick up rubbish and to give thanks, among other things. These are the powers of transformation. With these and similar powers, as others have observed, every life can be a testament, a window into a world of grace.

Part of the adventure of embracing a new direction in life is figuring out how to do it. As a neophyte runner, one of the first hurdles I had to jump was proper clothing. I discovered I needed clothes that pulled the sweat away from my body, yet loose enough so that I felt my body moving and alive in them. I don't like clinging Lycra shorts, even when double bagged with another pair of shorts to shield certain physical attributes from scrutiny.

Summer or winter I wear fully lined, generously fitted nylon running shorts, and a stippled polyester T-shirt made for running. In extreme cold I add a windbreaker. Then, toes liberally lubricated with Vaseline to prevent hot spots and blisters, I wear clean unwrinkled ankle socks and lace-up shoes. I'm not a barefoot runner, though I've read about it with curiosity and I admire my Melanesian friars who don't have much choice about it, but my feet are too tender. I fill my water bottle, and last of all I put on my cap. It is the finishing touch that makes me feel geared up for a run. It keeps the sun off my face, but has acquired layers of meaning so now the cap is almost a fetish cap, something I *must* wear. The more battered and sweat-stained the hat, the better – evidence of effort and with the animal funk of male power: ha!

As the days of running added up, I found myself celebrating nature's beauty and experiencing a physical and spiritual awakening; I was learning new ways of living in solidarity with other people too. I hope I was kinder and more caring of my brothers. I also became aware that before becoming sober, my social activism had a hint of anger, a dash of nastiness I directed at those who disagreed with me, or swallowed to keep the peace, allowing it to grow into an inner malignancy. Beginning to live differently, my social justice work became more congruent with my spiritual commitment. I became gentler, yet still on the lookout for practical ways to serve others. There are opportunities everywhere.

At a sharp bend in Pipe Stave Hollow Road, I pass an old house that I heard was once a station on the Underground Railroad. I can't find corroboration of this claim, except for the fact that the north shore of Long Island with its many inlets and wooded shoreline was favoured as a place to hide from slavers and to move on towards freedom in Canada. The Underground Railroad operated in the shadows, and I suspect the good that many people did may remain for ever between them, the people they helped and God.

I wondered what it would be like to be running for my life? To be a refugee? Whether or not the fact that the house was a station is historically accurate, there was a question that dug at my conscience. As I thought about escaped slaves, I wondered whether I would have had the temerity to risk life and limb to shelter runaway slaves? I prayed with all my heart I would.

Several years into my running practice, my prayers about the Underground Railroad and justice emboldened me to reach out to the Latino migrant workers on Long Island who were being harassed and persecuted. I found where the migrant workers met, which was in the basement of a restaurant. I contacted one of their leaders and volunteered to help in any way I could. I was handicapped by not speaking Spanish. But, I reasoned, God gave me this idea – I would see what happened.

Occasionally, they would ask me to march with them or tell their story in English at a rally. The workers didn't really need another Spanish-speaking rabble-rouser and advocate as much as they needed a local place to meet and organize themselves. Over the months that followed, Little Portion became a place of hospitality and refuge. Threatened with having our tax-exempt status revoked for helping 'illegal aliens', we prayed about this issue as a community. Finally, a senior brother summed up: 'I can't think of a better reason to lose our tax-exempt status.'

The brothers agreed to stand with the day labourers and offered our friary as a place to meet, come what may. The tax threats never came to pass. One evening over 100 young men showed up, in a long procession of cars and loud-farting trucks. They were organizing a soccer league as a way to bring their community together.

As a lark, one of our young Melanesian friars got into one of the teams. He couldn't communicate well with them verbally, but once on the field their common understanding of the game forged bonds of friendship. Laughter, high-fives, back slapping and sharing food and water were the principal ways they communicated off the field.

As a sign of appreciation for our hospitality the workers suggested they come one Sunday morning to clean up our friary gardens. With nearly 60 professional landscapers, that hour and a half transformed our ragged grounds. Then we all sat together and ate a lunch I had prepared, enjoying ourselves and stammering away in pidgin Spanglish. Though some spoke beautiful English, there weren't enough of these men to go around all the tables. Table fellowship made us brothers, no longer strangers or aliens. Perhaps it was a glimpse of the future, too: conversation at the heavenly banquet surely won't be limited by our human vocabularies.

As time went by, I marched, and prayed, and cooked food for them when they were evicted from their housing. I attracted the attention of the Suffolk County Executive, who referred to me and my worker-sympathizing colleagues, in a rhetorical flourish I will always cherish, as the 'lunatic fringe'.[2] Sadly, the conflict on Long Island intensified over the next few years and resulted in the death of a young immigrant.

At one point, we advertised 'micro-grants' to support local initiatives that dovetailed with some of our Franciscan values. Embodying our commitment to social justice and the joy of sport and play, we supported the workers' 20 football teams who were asking for money for first aid kits. One of the young players expressed the appreciation of his teammates: 'The brothers are the only ones who love us and want to be our friends.' Definitely not true – there were many others – but the heartfelt comment deepened our commitment to friendship and justice for these day labourers.

Cedar Beach, the turnaround point on my run, is exactly 3 miles from the friary door, per our car's odometer. Initially it seemed an unimaginable distance, in the same way that three months or years of sobriety was a daunting goal. I like to take a moment to savour this point of the run. I stand overlooking the pebbly beach, watching the waves and scanning the horizon. In summer, the beach is always filled with people who read or talk as children play at the water's edge. Lithe and beautiful lifeguards perch in their eyrie stands and watch more determined swimmers further out from shore.

When I have swum there in the summer, I love to float on my back, cosseted by the warmish water – like a child upon its mother's breast, as the psalmist says (Psalm 131.3, The Book of Common Prayer, p. 785). It is a taste of security and transcendence. During winter, the beach is dotted with heavily bundled walkers. One year I decided to go swimming on New Year's Day, starting a Franciscan Polar Bear Plunge. For several years after that, a group of brothers and our friends would splash into the icy waters on New Year's Day.

Talk about transcending! The point, I've always said, is to live New Year's Day as you want to live the rest of the year. I think living daringly, confounding expectations of comfort, making of life an adventure, even in a familiar neighbourhood, is a worthy ambition or resolution, even if it only lasts for a moment.

Taking a chance on God is not a one-time thing. Conversion of life is something that takes the whole of life. At the end of his life, St Francis said, 'Let us begin, brothers, to serve the Lord God, for up until now we have done little or nothing' (Thomas of Celano, 'The Life of St Francis', in Armstrong, Hellmann and Short, *Francis of Assisi*, vol. 1, p. 273). Open eyes and hearts, and new insights reveal a God at the heart of the world whose character is dynamic, evolving, changing, becoming. To become like this is our calling too.

Mahatma Gandhi, a personal hero of mine, advised experimentation with the truth. Some of his experiments were idiosyncratic, to say the least, yet he found his way to spiritual and political freedom. The goal is to become one's authentically true self, and thus capable of truly serving God and the earth and all peoples.

When I finally accepted that alcohol had betrayed my trust, and quit bellyaching and snivelling about it, I experienced sobriety breaking me out of a fear-based, anger-laced life. New horizons still loom: I am still called to let go of ways of living that have worked for a long time, in order to continue becoming the person God intends me to be.

There is no ducking the strangeness of my path through life so far. I sometimes feel so surprised to find myself as a grizzled athlete lacing up running shoes to head out into rain or snow flurries or slathering on sunblock to run in the tropical sun. The old questions of vocation come back: Who am I? What is God doing? What is the best way for me to respond? As my feet hit the road, fears slip away. I can do this, I can run the race that is set before me.

Notes

1 Institute for BioSpiritual Research, 'Why Biospiritual Focusing?' Available at: https://www.biospiritual.org/why-biospiritual-focusing/ (Accessed 5.12.16).

2 Southern Poverty Law Center, 'Climate of Fear: Latino Immigrants in Suffolk County, NY', 1 September 2009. Available at:www.splcenter.org/20090831/climate-fear-latino-immigrants-suffolk-county-ny (accessed 13.4.19)

2

Engaging the world differently: Snohomish, Washington

The Spirit is the God-ward dimension of the human being. It is not our ability to think or speak that enables us to engage with God. It is God's Spirit poured into us and entwining our own spirit that does that. (Gooder, *Body*, p. 80)

On a home visit, I look forward to running along Elliott Road, through spectacle-fogging mist hugging the stream that curls through the neighbour's farm, emptying into Lake Beecher. Long ago the Snohomish river abandoned this channel on its way to Puget Sound. It is now one of the wetlands in the Pacific Northwest.

This morning, as I run past, I am excited by grey herons startled out of the water, like spirits manifesting from the mist. The great birds' long-sighing cries send the beaver slap-tailing into the sloshy, grass-choked channels. Uprisings of squalling mallard ducks froth the water. Cattails are thick, growing from fleshy roots, tender shoots shove up beneath the growth of previous years. The old brown-furred heads explode with their woolly seeds. In season, ivory water lilies wink just out of reach. Blackberry canes ring the lake, in summer they are the image of abundance with each ebony drupelet impossibly fat. God's glory is manifested in exuberant life. Where no grass or reeds grow, the lake surface mirrors the sky: rain-rich clouds, dove grey and creamy white – occasionally, the bright blue of Northwest skies – and it makes me want to sing out loud.

This watery valley hugs my heart and imagination; to me it is evidence of the divine embrace of the world in its homely beauty and fecundity.

I am blessed that my parents have lived in the same house for over 50 years. Every year I wonder how much longer I will be able to return to my boyhood home, run across the fields around the house and visit neighbours I've known my whole life. I'm glad beyond telling every time I return home from my travelling life. I've given up trying to impress anybody around there with my growth and development. Perhaps for some of them I am still about 16 years old, balding, grey-stippled head notwithstanding. It's weird to glide beneath the calendar's radar. The real challenge can be navigating what I feel are my family's sometimes time-stuck responses to me. I have to remind myself not to forget and start reacting like a teenager: 'I'm a grown man! Leave it alone!' Not a mature come-back.

Humility, I read once, is about not justifying yourself, about not trying to escape what people think about you. The only way to change their perceptions is to live your truth. And if they persist in their own view, I don't need to force them to see me on my terms, just as I don't need to conform to their terms. Just live quietly and faithfully, try to enter their world (Richo, *When the Past is Present*, p. 173). My first running memory is of a time when I was about 13 or 14. My dad and my brother John and I endured a spate of macho fitness conditioning for several months. Dad would come into our room, and flick on the lights to rouse us from our bunk beds. 'Come on, boys! Good morning!' He was upbeat even at 5.30 a.m. Because it was dark and wet it must have been winter. For either Christmas or our February birthdays, we'd been presented with a bungee cord contraption that was supposed to build our muscles. Sleep-fogged and barely willing, I remember thrashing around like a fish on the dock. After several repetitions using this thing on arms, legs and back, we pulled on shoes and ran half a mile across the valley to a stop sign. I felt these early morning runs with my dad were exposing my inadequacies, and I hated them. I learned at school I was an Ichabod Crane, inept at sports. We slapped the stop sign post and ran back.

Shambling along behind my father, I prayed for invisibility, miserable beyond belief. Fortunately, it was a short-lived enthusiasm on Dad's part. I didn't develop an appreciation for those workouts for a long time. But now the memory of them has a roseate hue, my father's flailing runs marked a protective boundary, encircling my frightened spirit with his strong father's love. He couldn't take away my pain, the creeping sense of isolation I couldn't comprehend, but he did all in his power to show his solidarity.

More than anything else, I think he wanted to connect with his sons – and my sisters too, though they weren't part of these early morning exercise sessions. He wanted to encourage us to be active and fit as we matured, as much as he hoped we'd be loving, compassionate, reliable people. Those runs are the reason I often 'touch base' at turnaround points in my runs today: a gesture of gratitude and solidarity with my young father.

There is a memory of a night run that I don't know what to do with. I must have been about 16 years old, in the days when streakers made the national newspapers. Unable to sleep one night, I stripped off my night clothes, heart hammering in my chest. I needed to get outside. An imperative urge: to be outside, running in the dark. Was I fleeing from erotic thoughts and feelings? Seeking to embrace a wildness, a dive through a liminal place? Perhaps it was the call of my emerging masculine identity, a test against my comfortable youth or an intuited rite of passage?

Naked, I ran into the dark, slipping and sliding through the wet underbrush that reached out with stinging thorns, and jabbing twigs. I splashed through the stream at the foot of the ravine and up on to the county road. The stony paving bruised my feet. I ran unthinkingly, blindly, through the dark. When the headlights of cars probed the dark around me, I hid in the undergrowth, gasping air.

Hunkered under the thimbleberry bushes, sweat trickled down my back, the smell from damp earth and bruised leaves a thick vegetal fug. My erection was a precious thing I shielded with my hand. What was I doing? I came home exultant with bruised feet, mud-streaked thighs, bleeding arms. I slipped past the light from my parents' bedroom, crouched along the edge of the lawn. The lacy, wet and fragrant red cedar branches slapped against my face, stroked my back.

Never repeated, I remember recounting my night time run to a therapist. He didn't say a word, only watched me, eyes bright with interest.

Running on home turf, I have often recalled the struggles of being a gay boy, feeling isolated, damaged. Rambling in the woods and lakes, I sought a sense of connection and solace. Through the ferns and berry bushes, spying out the hollowed stumps of once majestic trees, I would pick my way fantasizing I was a pioneer, or a trapper – somebody who was cut off from the rest of humanity, and self-reliant. There were some particularly big stumps and I could crawl into one, and pretend it was a fort, or imagine building a roof on it and creating my own hobbit house. Mostly, I wanted a place where nobody teased me, where it didn't matter if I couldn't catch a ball. Me against the world. I'd have paid a king's ransom to have a friend my own age.

Manhood and sexual identity at 16 were a giddy, terrifying scramble. Now in middle age I am discovering a communion with other men that I've longed for all my life; the subject of our talks and laughter was beyond me as a youth. It is from reflection on the different paths we have followed in life – our fears, disappointments and persistent hopes and satisfactions – that I have anything to talk about. Thank God it is less about ball games or car engines or girls, the three things boys in Snohomish used to talk about, topics about which I had less than no interest at the time. Experience of the world and a greater sense of self-confidence have given me a few toss-off lines even on these subjects. In the area of human attraction, however, I finally feel free enough not to lie.

I remember vividly when David Kopay, the Seattle football player, told his coming-out story as a gay man and athlete to the Seattle newspaper in 1975 when I was a senior in high school. I waited for those articles and read them avidly. Once my mother saw me standing in the front hallway reading about it in the newspaper: 'Are you reading the sports pages?' she asked incredulously. 'No!' I said, crumpling it quickly, flushed with anxiety and guilt. 'No, I'm not.' I found his story fascinating and deeply disturbing.

When I was 26, ordained a deacon and engaged to be married, I unburdened my conscience in confession. Mumbling in a strangled voice, I told about my experiments with same-sex encounters, fearing I would be fiercely chastised. To my utter surprise the priest demanded: 'Answer me. Do you think you are truly gay? If you are, you must accept yourself, and welcome this identity as God's gift to you.' It was a challenge to an integrated life, one that it would take me several years to face squarely. We broke off the engagement. I remember feeling terrified of what might become of me. It was at the height of the AIDS epidemic, and I was living in New York. I had panic attacks thinking about how I could ever accept this so-called gift.

Discovery of ourselves, learning who we are, how we might live in the world, begins in infancy, and it doesn't seem to be over at 59. It's an endurance race of a different order. As a young man, I tried on different attitudes and values like changes of clothing. As I grew older, I found I had some core issues, and at each new stage in my life they have required renewed attention: finding friends, sharing intimacy, learning to be at home in the world, to be content with who I am, helping others.

Thinking about sexuality I usually think about vocation, too. The two are inextricably linked in my mind, both part and parcel of God's embrace. They are two of the recurrent themes in my running meditations. I am always engaging them, then letting go. Hopefully, they will be resolved by living my life more than by trying to figure them out. I am learning to trust myself and God. When I joined the friars, I had three reasons for doing so. First of all, I wanted to live a more radical Christian life in service and worship. I wanted to live and work more closely with the poor, in a life fundamentally shaped by liturgy and Scripture. The second reason was that I fell in love with Francis. Reading about him in a book given to me tumbled me into endless reveries and daydreams, not unlike other infatuations I'd had. I wanted to be like him, to share his life in whatever way possible. It was his courage to conform to Christ and be himself against all social conventions that I admired. And the third reason I joined the friars was that I was lonely. I wanted family, community life. The fact that many of the friars were gay men was appealing. It was after I joined that I had the courage to speak about my sexual identity. The brothers helped me and supported me. Early on, one brother circled my waist with an arm and said: 'I sure hope you get used to being gay pretty soon. It would be good to hear you talk about something else.'

I wish I could say it was easily done, but the process included some faltering steps. There was to be a lot of confusion and tears. But the brothers were never anything but accepting of my struggle to accept my sexuality. Coming out in a celibate religious order felt like Odysseus lashed to the mast as he sailed past the Sirens (see Homer, *The Odyssey, Book XII*). The ties that bound me were the still-strong feelings of a vocation to be a friar. To be a deeply committed, honest, gay friar. That was my prayer.

Nick Benton, early in the collection of his essays *Extraordinary Hearts*, writes:

[S]ame sex erotic attraction is the embodiment of a socio-physical impulse of self-development, a manifestation of the very nature of the universe and the evolution of humanity toward equality, justice, and ultimately love in its truest form. As such … this view sees same sex erotic attraction as at its core Promethean, as that which gives life and progress to humanity as transformative and revolutionary. Thus, it is not a variant or a deviation of the heterosexual impulse for biological reproduction. It is an expression of our species' natural impulse for preservation and advancement through social, not biological reproduction. (p. 30)

Prometheus was the Greek god who was creator of humanity, and he gave the gift of fire stolen from Olympus. Benton goes on in his astounding essay to critique the hedonistic 'sex is everything' approach to gay life he saw in the 1970s and 1980s. He traces this same-sex-attraction life-force in the work of Eleanor Roosevelt, Walt Whitman, and many others. Benton celebrates the giftedness inherent in being gay in his description of gay sensibility that promotes art, beauty, justice and peace. Having genital sex is not the sole defining characteristic of being gay. My justice-based, beauty-inflected, spiritually hungry gay identity naturally informs my vocation. Of course, the same must be said about heterosexuals with vocations: their sexuality is God's gift to them, too. The wonderful thing is to claim, without shame or deceit, the gifts of God for our happiness and for the healing of the world in Jesus' name.

With same-sex marriage equality, the celibate commitment of religious life is finally revealed in the bright light of freedom. While celibacy is no longer the only sanctioned choice for gay Christians, embracing celibacy is a reckoning of what works, what fits a person's personality, how one intuits the best way to shape a life. Some try celibacy and discover it is not for them. I think some are called to it for a time, others for life. Nor is celibacy merely an ecclesiastical requirement. I have known celibate atheists – you can't blame celibacy entirely on the Church. My maxim is: follow the joy!

Trouble can arise when celibacy is a requirement for ordination and ministry. This is not the case for Episcopal priests, though it is a requirement of Franciscan brothers in the Episcopal Church. The decision to be a friar is partly how I decided to order my private life. Not having sex doesn't mean I think sex is bad or wrong. It is renunciation, *not* rejection, as Laurence Freeman OSB helpfully characterizes the lifestyle choice and vocation of the teachers of the desert in the fifth century (Introduction to Williams, *Silence and Honey Cakes*, p. 9). Celibate religious life is not a closet, but a vantage-point from which to understand and serve the world. Everyone discerning such a choice must reckon honestly with the real sense of invitation to a beautiful, very different life.

Not every run at home begins with a heavy meditation on sexuality and vocation, but these matters are signposts for me of familiar spiritual territory with roots going deep into my earliest memories.

I have always felt surrounded by a great crowd of friends, the living and departed, on this run through home territory. At the foot of the driveway is a sign: 'Tenas Illihee', carved by my grandfather. He insisted it means 'Little Home' in the nineteenth-century Chinook trading jargon of western Washington.

On this route, I run past our neighbours' small farm holdings and across the valley to the old dairy farm. When we first moved there in 1965, the farm was leased and operated by a German émigre doctor and his wife; another neighbour had warned us about bothering them, so we stayed away. But a year or so later the doctor died. After church on Thanksgiving Day, my dad took us kids to visit our neighbour while the turkey was roasting in the oven because his heart was stirred by the Epistle reading for the day from the Letter of James about visiting widows.

As we walked up the drive, we were greeted with open arms by Herta, one of the loveliest people imaginable. She cried out a greeting and asked why we'd never come before. They had watched our house being built and wondered what kind of people we were. We invited her and her German farm assistant,

Peter, to come over that evening. And they did so in evening clothes, dress and tuxedo, which sent my father and grandfather rushing to their rooms for ties and jackets. They became instant friends of the family.

We shifted irrigation pipes with them in the summer and then enjoyed ice cream in the farm kitchen. At Christmas, she had a small tree decorated with candles, tinsel and apples. Within a few years of that first Thanksgiving, the farm was sold, and the doctor's widow moved to Washington DC to teach liturgical dance with her sister. Peter moved to another farm, yet we always maintained close ties.

We adopted Peter as an uncle. He had been a young boy during World War Two and served in the Hitler Youth; then he was sent to a Russian prisoner-of-war camp. When he returned home, his family's estate had been destroyed, and he fled with them to the West. Eventually, he arrived alone in rural Washington State. During all my teenage years, he was a frequent visitor. In time, another German man, Hans, became a close family friend. Hans was Jewish and fought with the Americans in the war. Hans and Peter took an instant liking to each other. Hans was the concert master for the opera company in town, and Peter loved opera. I remember listening to them laugh and argue. Hans had a knack for embracing any argument with a laugh and his favourite exclamation: 'Fantastic!' When I remember Peter and Hans, I laugh: 'Fantastic!' With a personalist approach to life triumphing over ideology, prejudice, shame, anger, those men helped in creating a new world in the shell of the old, as Peter Maurin wrote in one of his *Easy Essays* (p. 109); a chosen world glittering with art and beauty around our dinner table, where sorrow and loss were healed by joy, understanding, forgiveness and friendship. From them I learned that we choose to make of life what we will; we can bring good from even horrendous circumstances.

The friendly and entrepreneurial family who bought the farm have owned it ever since. It had been a showplace dairy and now is a sweetcorn and pumpkin Mecca. Memories of wet grass and cowpats come back as I run by the farm.

It is a hard sprint up a steep incline off Elliott Road to Fales Road. I have to edge around a blind corner where a western red cedar grows directly from the edge of the asphalt and cars cut as close to the tree as possible. I have always been ready to spring on to the steep hillside, into the nettles and brambles, if need be. But it has never happened, thank God. On the higher ground are a series of equine farms, people I never got to know. There's a dog along there, and I have learned to keep a wary eye out for it. Increasingly, over the years as it's aged, it has stayed behind the fence rails, barking defiantly. I don't know why the creature bothers, I only want to get away as quickly as possible.

Calamity Hill is an unmapped, peculiar family landmark. My dad had an accident coming over the crest of the unnamed knoll a bit fast and had to swerve into the ditch to avoid hitting a car that was stopped on the other side, the motorist talking with a cyclist. Running up the steep incline, I found myself remembering the calamities of my life, weighing them against the struggles I've made to change.

Some of us as young adults – gay or straight – struggled a lot with shame and sought love in all the wrong places. I tried to fill the Grand Canyon inside of me with alcohol. It was an unconscious thing. I noticed when I drank that I seemed to have more friends, that I was funnier, that I could take risks in relating to others that I never could when sober. It was a fool's paradise. Eventually I had to swerve into a ditch too. Thank God, I never killed anybody nor caused permanent damage to myself.

The motivation for change has been to find relief from the pain of the consequences of my drinking. The drinking and its fallout – broken friendships, fear, lying – are common or garden calamities when compared with the circumstances of refugees from war or people dying of starvation. I've learned it is pointless to compare myself to others. Overcoming the shame that we feel about our actions can liberate us for a more profound engagement with life.

Recovery is full of slogans, and one always catches my attention: 'Religion is for those who are afraid of hell, spirituality is for those who have been to hell and back.' I don't quibble with the sentiment, only holding out for myself the reminder that 'religion' means to 'bind together'. It is supposed to be a cohesive, strengthening, uniting force. When do we start to reclaim that?

I had hoped, in a dim, vague way, that the religious community would take care of all my needs, and somehow absolve me of my failings. Magical thinking. Religious community doesn't absolve you of anything or take care of all your needs; but the ache for wholeness has prompted my prayer, and there are enough sweet tastes of joy and healing for me.

Religious life isn't perfect, but good enough. I am given many chances for prayer, and if I am brave and honest, the chance to reflect deeply on my life. From that deep reflection, I can honestly say that the people supporting me in religious life waited for the penny to drop, for the realization to come to me that I needed help with my drinking. Then they could support me more effectively.

Family, sober friends, and my Franciscan brothers have supported me, sometimes just by giving me space to be myself and accepting me. Once an older friar told me he loved me. I hugged the blessing in my heart for days.

The relationships of depth and intimacy I feel with some of the brothers are as precious as the fine pearls hidden in the field Jesus talks about. Sell everything and go and get those pearls! Being a friar is many times better than anything I had before. A friend has written challengingly that healthy adults can expect to have only 25 per cent of their needs met by other people. Most of the soothing, support, and affirmation comes from within (Richo, *Daring to Trust*, p. 24). From God, I believe.

As I run, I wonder and pray about these wounds and memories and how they shaped my life. I run because of joy, grace befriending my self-identity. Not Ichabod but a son of Prometheus: 'You are gods,' the Lord says, 'all of you children of the Most High' (Psalm 82.6, Book of Common Prayer). I slap the sign for Downes Road, my turnaround point.

I stop to soak in the smells of the meadow, the spice of the cedars, a mist prickles my face, and steam rises off my hot body. My body and spirit are fully engaged. 'With all that I am and all that I have I honour you, Lord God.' I pray with St Augustine: 'You have made [me] for yourself and [my] heart is restless until it rests in you' (*Confessions I.1*, p. 3). From the running and the many memories of my youth have come fullness and blessing.

3

Cracking the imagination open:
Honiara: Solomon Islands

[St Paul teaches that] presenting our bodies to God involves placing who we are and what we do into his care and keeping. Once we do that it becomes imperative that we do not allow our minds to be moulded by this age – the old creation that will pass away – and all its concerns ... The renewal of our minds involves ongoing transformation inside so that our lives can be transfigured ... Inner transformation revealed in outer transfiguration is what Paul appears to have in mind ... (Gooder, *Body*, p. 106)

Awakened in the middle of the night in Patteson House, Honiara, in the Solomon Islands, I often heard bottles broken, people screaming at one another. The heavy bass beating from car stereos and a nearby disco made the glass louvres buzz in the window. 'Welcome to the tropical paradise of the Happy Isles,' I often groused to myself. Sheets clung to my sweaty body, kamikaze mosquitoes dive bombed my chest, sometimes another insect spelunked my nose. Equatorial nights can be long. This is real life, on its own terms.

I remember a friend driving me in her car one day after I announced to my parish in Tacoma, Washington, back in the States that I would be leaving to join the Society of St Francis. She was a very supportive friend, and yet my choice concerned her. She said how sorry she was that I would be 'leaving the world'. I was leaving the rat race, I hoped, but hardly the world.

'Leaving the world' is used by Franciscans to signify detachment from the anaesthetizing values that have driven society for centuries: capitalism and militarism, to name two. Friars try to be non-cooperative in the gun-wielding, waste-producing, car-driving, power-mad world we know today. I was delighted to draw a line in the sand.

But even then, I knew I wasn't leaving the world *per se*. I would still be caught up in all the ordinary aspects of life. I would need to work at a job, cook, clean, preach, cope with traffic – in an ageing Geo Metro – and deal with the life of the Church. I expected to approach it from within a community that questioned middle-class American life. I never imagined, though, the degree to which my life would involve a head-first dive into pain and vulnerability, simple joy and beauty, and trying to keep my mind off what other people around me are thinking or doing. I haven't left any world except a fantasy world.

Is it 'leaving the world' when you live in a hot climate without air-conditioning or hot showers? And have virtually no control over who comes into your house? Even my friary in New York was like a bus station with strangers coming and going. You are expected to eat whatever is put in front of you. People reach out, asking for help, advice, comfort, a word of prayer wherever you go – is that leaving the world? I wonder if our First World amenities don't insulate us from the world. Frankly, I think the wealthy with their air-conditioning, automatic-locking luxury cars, gated communities and private clubs, overstocked supermarkets, instant communications technology, have left the world farther behind than any God-stricken friar.

At 5.30 a.m. most mornings in Honiara, the wake-up call of the parish's large wooden drum reverberates through the neighbourhood. Remembering stories about how Native Americans communicated by drums, and recalling comments about talking drums among African peoples, one morning I asked a brother who was pounding on the hollowed-out log what the message was he was sending, for the rhythm was the same every morning in all the places I visited. 'Get out of bed and come to church!' he said. The nagging drum was followed 15 minutes later by the clangour of a bell – an aesthetic improvement over the more common practice of a piece of steel being hammered on an empty propane gas tank. It meant 15 minutes until morning Mass at All Saints' Church.

The morning rituals finish with the Franciscans gathering in their cupboard-like chapel built over the toilet block. We say our own morning prayers, listen to a reading of a chapter of the Rule. Then, after we have shaken hands with one another, I go to my room and prepare upcoming talks and lesson plans while the brothers and other men around the friary grab brooms of bundled coconut leaf ribs and start the daily tidying of the grounds. The skritch-skritch of the brooms and the belch of heavy vehicles mingle together: morning has broken again, Honiara-style. Leaves, blossoms like fallen stars, food wrappers and other detritus are kicked into piles. Outside the perimeter fence the brothers patrol for rubbish. It is a disheartening, Sisyphean task, as the moment they have cleaned up the area, it is filthy again as the wind pilfers from the litter bins. Acrid-smelling smoke from burning piles of plastic waste wafts here and there in the neighbourhood. The inadequate litter bins and the dilatory municipal rubbish collection service are the trouble. This is obvious, for as soon as the bins are emptied, crowds of people almost immediately fill them again. But the brothers do what they can, keeping their side of the street as clean as possible.

Singing and laughter burble around. Brothers call out to friends. Early visitors to the friary sit on the benches along the outside wall talking, chewing betel nut. Many of them are just off the ships that dock close by at the town wharf after an overnight passage, or many days' passage, from other islands. Their cargo lies heaped on the ground around their bare feet, plastic-wrapped or bundled in leaves and vine roping. Finally, we eat breakfast, either a packet of ship's biscuits or a stack of four slices of white bread from the dizzily fragrant Hot Bread Company at the crossroads, with tea or instant coffee.

Patteson House was built in 1971 as our urban friary in the Solomon Islands. It was the first religious house shared by men and women religious from different communities in the Anglican Communion, the brothers of the Society of St Francis and the sisters of the Community of the Sisters of the Church. Originally, membership of both communities was made up of European and Melanesian members living together; now they are entirely Melanesian. The sisters' side has a feminine shine. Meals are regular and balanced. The rooms are cleaned with panache by the sisters, raised from birth in the domestic arts.

The brothers, by contrast, are 'army', as they call it. Food is simpler, often rougher. For instance, bones and scales are left in the fish when cooked and served. Life is altogether more *ad hoc*. They can chop wood like the legendary giant Paul Bunyan but overlook dirty windows – or windows without the glass louvres. I never turn down an invitation to eat with the sisters – nor do the other brothers. Relations between the two sides are warm and friendly, very definitely sibling relationships. Their familiarity with one another is like any other group of people who live together: collegial and antagonistic, indulgent and spiteful – but loving over all. Sisters and brothers.

The starting brief for these two communities with European origins was urban ministry, serving seafarers, schools, prisoners, offering hospitality to people coming to town. Over the years, the Sisters of the Church took the lead in developing a powerful ministry to women fleeing domestic abuse, and they established the Christian Care Centre. Now it is a project supported by all four of the Anglican religious orders in the Church of Melanesia. It is chiefly run by sisters from the two women's communities, the Community of the Sisters of the Church and the Community of the Sisters of Melanesia, but the Franciscan brothers and members of the Melanesian

Brotherhood are involved with maintenance, security and developing a programme called Male Advocates, working with the abusive men.

The Franciscan brothers offer hospitality at Patteson House to great numbers of people every day, many gathering in the traditional leaf-roofed kitchen built on the slope behind the house. This backyard kitchen is like a small community centre. Its mud floor and bamboo walls are blackened by daily fires. Conga lines of ants shimmy over the benches. I was once bitten on the testicles, to general amusement and speculation about the interesting lives of ants as I hopped about, clawing at myself. Hunkered in their man cave, the brothers and many other male visitors smoke cigarettes made of homegrown tobacco called *sau-sau* and rolled with newspaper or notebook paper. They drag on these over a juicy quid of betelnut, the peppery, clove-like betel-nut flavour mingling delectably with the tobacco smoke. But it leaves many of them toothless, with red-stained mouths.

While abstaining from these chemical pleasures, I tried to spend time each day sprawled on the rough benches, 'storying', as I obsessively crushed the ants marching on my legs and my inviting baggy brown uniform shorts. Some of our residents are homeless and drug-addicted. Some are village men who, with their sons or grandsons, are needing relatively long-term accommodation. Some are students or who-knows-what, just staying overnight. At night, a dozen or so men bed down on woven mats on the dining room's concrete floor and brothers often allow their male relatives to share their rooms. When my brother, John, came to visit me from America, the brothers gave me an extra mattress. There was no question about where he was staying. My brother and I had a great time, laughing and whispering all night like we used to do as young boys. Six friars are assigned to live at Patteson House, but nearly 18 men gather for breakfast and dinner each day. It is a relief to slip through the gates and run for a time away from this Mad Hatter tea party of Melanesian men.

Running in any urban environment is less pleasurable for me than a rural one. On a Honiara run, exhaust fumes, tricky pavements and mushy patches of rubbish create an obstacle course. I feel wary and on guard. Breathing seems more difficult. By 9.30 on a typical morning, the early morning market trucks and buses have come and gone – the rush hour is over – and that's when I head out for a run. I pick my way through the glass-spangled area in front of the bottle shop. The shattered bottles recall the nocturnal cacophony.

I can remember my own years of late-night carousing, breaking bottles, shouting irresistible witticisms, feeling superior. I never want to forget that time, the easy relinquishment of mindfulness, dignity and charity. As a blackout drinker, I tried to disbelieve the tales of hurt and degradation my drinking pals told me about. I keep the door to these distressing memories propped open to remind myself where I have come from and where I could fall back to, if I should ever start drinking again.

Now a sober friar and a runner, nothing stands between me and those drinkers except prayer. If I stopped praying, I'd very likely be drinking again, and not running. I thank God for the healing that running and prayer have brought to my life, and my growing ability to accept and work with the challenges that come at me during sober living.

In Honiara, my route goes beneath the shadow of a steep hill. Above me, at the top of the hill, stands the iconic House of Parliament with its round teepee-like roof. The local papers are strident in their critique of government, and they diagnose the nation's ills as due in large part to corruption. There is no secret about it. But the challenge is in mustering the political power to change the system that owes much to the traditional *wantok* system that favours friends and relatives. Corruption is a common topic of conversation. The challenge for them, and citizens the world over, is to move from critique to action. In the meantime, it is a lesson about living in that in-between, liminal reality of life-as-it-really-is.

As James Hillman writes:

we must be clear that to live or love only where one can trust, where there is security and containment, where one cannot be hurt or let down, where what is pledged in words is forever binding, means really to be out of harm's way and so to be out of real life. And it does not matter what is this vessel of trust – analysis, marriage, church or law, any human relationship. (Hillman, *Loose Ends*, cited by David Richo in a handout at Advent Retreat 2015, San Damiano Friary, San Francisco)

In recovery I am frequently chivvied to 'live life on life's terms' – which means to let go of a host of controlling behaviours as well as to fight corruption and environmental squalor one step at a time, not pining for 'somebody' to 'do something'.

Along my route there are many signs of development in Honiara: new hotels, casinos, government buildings. These are flickers of hope for a stable society to develop. Trying to build an infrastructure in a country of only half a million people, many of whom are subsistence farmers or fishermen, must be daunting in the extreme. Australia is a hugely generous aid provider, as are Taiwan, South Korea and Japan. Australia provided the Regional Assistance Mission to the Solomon Islands (RAMSI) after the ethnic-tension fighting rocked the tiny nation in 1999–2004. There are still Australian military types around, and I am sometimes mistaken for one when I run.

As I run around the corner at Rove, I pass the prison. The razor wire fencing and guards are the same everywhere in the world. None the less, this is a small facility, ringed by stately palms and tropical vegetation; it's not Riker's Island, the site of a tough New York prison. A brother goes to Rove Prison frequently to visit and pray with the inmates. Br Hilton and I once did a Bible study there. We went to the maximum-security section, where many of the militants from the ethnic tension convicted of crimes are serving their time.

After shaking hands with everybody, we sang with the men

and shared our Bible study. As we were leaving, Hilton filled me in on the prison ministry. 'Sometimes,' he said, 'we go and visit Harold Keke.'

Harold was a leader of some militants who had killed seven members of the Melanesian Brotherhood. He is in prison for life. I was deeply moved. 'What's that like?' I asked. 'Is it hard to be with the murderer of your brothers?' They were extremely grisly murders, too, with evidence of torture. Hilton admitted that at first he was deeply ambivalent. He tapped his head to indicate Keke was possibly mentally ill. 'Harold needs help and prayers, too,' my brother told me. Hilton and the brothers kept visiting him solely because Jesus said to do so. For the brothers, who were non-partisan in the struggle and served as peacemakers, the past is forgiven. During the conflict, they prayed with all the militants, trying in their inimitable Melanesian way to bring the fighters to their senses. The prayers have had a big impact in the prison, too. One young former militant and confrere of Keke's joined our community after serving nine years in prison. He's still under 30 and volunteers for all the hard jobs in the friary. He sits quietly among the brothers. Sometimes his shoulders are slumped, arms akimbo like the wings of a wounded bird. One day I asked him about his life, and he said he just wanted so desperately to make it right.

The past can be a latent threat. Like a court order in a file drawer. Or what might be revealed by a Google search. Or like a shark in the depths of the sea. For no apparent reason, old actions, acquaintances, statements can suddenly emerge from murky depths to attack you in the present moment. In early sobriety, my greatest desire was to shout them down. I wanted to prove I was a good person, worthy of trust. I worked hard, perhaps taking on too many jobs. I remember sitting with a brother on the porch in New York, and he asked me, very gently: 'Do you feel you have to make up for your mistakes?' I nodded yes, but I couldn't answer. Tears stung my eyes and emotion swelled my throat.

Eventually I got through that phase of my recovery. I can't

possibly make up for what I did, but I can live differently today, and establish a new track record. Because of my past, I am who I am, so I can even be grateful for it. What counts is my willingness to change. As the Principles of our Order state: humility, love and joy – and I'd add forgiveness – are all supernatural graces that can be won only from the divine bounty.

Running from Rove to Bishop's Court, home of the Anglican Archbishop of the Church of Melanesia, I push on for the last mile or so to White River Bridge. Perched on the bridge's scuffed and red betel-juice-stained balustrade, I watch the rubbish-choked stream under it and the traffic passing by me, waving to people I know, and drinking slowly from my water bottle. The first few times I ran in the tropics after becoming Minister General, I was dismayed at how hard it was to cover relatively short distances. I found I was exhausted and stumbling after 3 miles. At home that was nothing.

But when I began running, I hadn't always bothered to drink water. In the tropics, I learned it is imperative. I remember once when I was feeling weak and exhausted another runner asking me with some concern and a touch of impatience: 'Are you drinking water?' Well, actually… no, I hemmed and hawed. 'Hell, you're dehydrated, susceptible to sunstroke and getting sick,' my friend told me. I sheepishly agreed. I now carry a water bottle everywhere I run. It makes all the difference. 'The water of life' is not just a metaphor.

Not far from the bridge is St Francis Church, White River. I've preached there a couple of times, once on Easter Sunday. I think nearly 500 people were crowded around that Easter morning – as many as could squeeze into the iron-roofed church. The rest pressed against the windows from outside. The windows are large, without glass, so everybody could hear if I shouted. Perched on bouncy plank benches, people fanned themselves, eyes fixed on the sanctuary. I felt anxiety nibbling ant-like in my belly. I'd decided to talk about getting sober. I told them a part of my story of coming to sobriety, inviting them to think of the power of the resurrection in their lives. 'It is not just my story,' I said. The power of getting sober with other people who are also struggling to become sober is, in the words of Wendell Berry, 'the story of lives knit together, overlapping in succession, rising again from grave after grave' ('Rising', *New Collected Poems*, p. 277). Sharing in the resurrection of Jesus is about salvation, allowing God to unlock our imaginations to look at the world differently. Christianity teaches that on Easter morning we are to celebrate our life as redeemed by God from the bondage of death: our life, and the life of our communities, the life of the Church and the world. When Jesus met Mary Magdalene on that first Easter morning, the unimaginable took place. Who could imagine somebody rising from the dead? The story challenges us to consider the shutdown places in our lives, the parts we feel cannot be changed, and imagine them transformed. If you can imagine it, you can live it.

Jesus stands at those crossroads calling us each by name. 'Mary,' he said, and she suddenly recognized him. 'Francis.' 'Paul.' 'Joanna.' 'Clark.' When I heard my name one hot June afternoon, I was waking up on a train seat where I'd passed out after drinking, sun burning my face. It was a peculiar moment of clarity, one I never anticipated: I realized that my life must change because I was on an accelerating downward spiral. The sealed-off 'leave me alone' attitude was like spiritual solitary confinement. I was getting buried alive.

What happened in my life was a spiritual revolution, a change in body and spirit: putting down the drink is Easter at any time of the year. I learned new ways to pray, I began to see myself and the world with gratitude. New life was no longer just a theological argument, but a sweaty, sometimes difficult, yet laughter-filled reality. An Easter People needs to pray through the fears that stop us. We are sent out to the people around us, as Jesus sent Mary Magdalene to the disciples, to shake the cages people live in.

Cage-shaking is a worthy calling. Franciscans could do more

of it. When I was Protestant chaplain at Stony Brook University, the poet Robert Bly advised a group of students to smash up their televisions, and to take up pens, brushes, what-have-you, and create! I would add: Go for a walk, start to jog, even if just downhill. Get into nature somehow.

For years, I relied on alcohol for my excitement, though I always felt frustrated when I couldn't remember half of what I'd done as I 'partied'. We are capable of more than we think without alcohol or drugs of any kind to give us a high. The reserves of imagination lie below the surface, often untapped. All it takes is the smallest effort to see the world from a different perspective. A real natural high.

One of the most liberating and empowering changes for me in recovery was a determination not to see the world solely in all-or-nothing terms. I was not too old to start running, for example. Nor is it too hot to run, if you pace yourself slowly and drink water. And it is generally possible to find something to admire in most people I meet.

As I retraced my steps to the friary through the western suburbs of Honiara, along the crumbling pavement, through mud puddles, around piles of rubbish, I also noticed the frangipani blossoms, the new buildings, the smiles of vendors. Life is never completely bad. There is beauty and goodness to be registered and delighted in, even as we commit ourselves to fighting the bad things.

Once, after several weeks touring friaries on other islands, I was back in town, recuperating from the boat trip and preparing for my departure to New Zealand. The sea travel had been rough: normally a six-hour trip, we'd laboured on for over eight hours. Slugged by wind-whipped waves and stung by rain, the boat had grovelled and gurgled in the sea. At one point the captain had shouted for us to gather on one side to balance the shifting cargo; we caused the ship to tip alarmingly. A woman clung to my arm: 'We're going to drown!' she wailed – then promptly vomited over me. I was grateful to be off the scow and alive.

As I did my laundry in a bucket, our 3-ton truck lumbered into the side yard of Patteson House. The postulants and novices jumped off the back, they had come to see me off. It had been nearly three weeks since my visit to the training house, Hautambu. It was wonderful to see these young men again; they crowded around to shake my hand. 'How, brother?' I asked one. 'All right?'

'Yeah!' he said enthusiastically. 'I go running every day! Your visit shook us up. Now every brother runs, every day!' The others laughed: 'Yes, brother! We go out every afternoon before prayer.' I saw them waking up, engaging, taking responsibility for their own lives and wellbeing, a stance that could only have a positive impact on community life.

In a Franciscan leadership workshop, I'd called on them to ground their Franciscan vocation by using their warrior spirit – their protective, creative energy that their traditional culture teaches is the gift of young manhood to the community. Part of the joy of working with them is claiming that warrior spirit myself; running is one of the ways I work at that. As Matthew Fox says: 'We have to work at our true identity, and this is part of the warrior's work: To be strong in who we are, who we are becoming, what we stand for, what the values we cherish are that call us forward into new places, new roles' (*Sins of the Spirit*, p. 252).

The warrior spirit is not a war-like spirit, but a fierceness, a commitment rooted in faith to our values and the communities to which we belong. As Paula Gooder says, becoming who we are meant to be requires inner transformation, a waking up from obsessive behaviours, and showing it forth through outer transfiguration. Jesus simply said, 'Let your light shine.' To 'walk the talk' is the age-old challenge of living with integrity. In recovery, the warrior's challenge is tempered by the realistic counsel that we are seeking spiritual progress, not perfection. Perfectionism can be a mental and spiritual trap that sometimes threatens to overwhelm me even after 18 years of sobriety.

4

Following the God of compassion: Hautambu, Solomon Islands

The real 'me' is to be found in the entirety of my being rooted and grounded in the love of and relationship with Christ. (Gooder, *Body*, p. 96)

As the truck crested the hill at Kesao on the rutted, dusty road from Honiara, the capital of the Solomon Islands, I could see Hautambu in the distance around the curving shore near Veranaaso. The name 'Hautambu' means All Souls. The traditional belief is that the souls of the dead gather at this craggy, wave-licked tip of the island before departing for the afterlife. The friary there, perched on the hilltop, is a training house for the novices of the Province of the Solomon Islands. It is still a launching place for souls. Young men come to seek God's will and go out into the world with the message of Christian love. All that is visible of Hautambu from the truck are the silhouettes of palm trees bowing to kiss the sea. It is an ever-changing tableau of clouds and waves, like the inspired inventions of a restless child stacking blocks of cloud, scattering white shards of waves. Seeing this view, I have always felt a quickening within me, a feeling in my stomach of entering a home zone, even though it's on the other side of the earth from my birthplace. The Solomon Islands wade into the South Pacific off the east coast of Australia, just south of the equator. There are two or three places in the world where I have an intense feeling of homecoming, and La Verna Friary at Hautambu is one of them. The glimpse from Kesao packs the punch of glancing at a photo of a beloved. This tropical home offers me unaffected welcomes and the familiar routines of religious community: prayer, daily meetings called chapters, communal work and study, simple hospitality. Plenty of laughter and fun. Part of the appeal is also that it is a place to connect with some of the basic rhythms of a life totally different from my American upbringing. These rhythms are intriguing and satisfying: farming with machetes, cooking over fire, laundry done in a bucket or in the river, relaxing with a bitter quid of betel nut tucked into my cheek.

As the truck descended into the old Roman Catholic settlement, where the missionaries first came to Guadalcanal, the water was lost to sight. Soon we approached Paru, and I saw the large mango tree that is the eastern terminus of my usual running route. I figured out I was now close enough to Hautambu to get there on my own if the truck should fail. This concern is not far-fetched, the friary vehicles are old and break down regularly, and need to be worked on furiously between trips to town.

I think this friary was one of the first places I ever felt accepted and admired without caveat, enveloped in a warm community of men eager to be around me. Of course, I was a big white foreigner as exotic as a snowflake to these young men, but when I first went to live there for nearly 11 months from September 1995 until July 1996, I found a niche in their community life. The dial of the combination lock on my heart clicked gently into place, letting the door open. I came to feel an intimacy with some of the brothers at Hautambu that was greater than anywhere else outside my home. Here I had 40 young brothers to care for, and they cared for me: there was a sense of an unclenching and relaxing into emotional and physical closeness.

I had learned celibate friendship as primarily talking, sharing confidences from time to time. My Melanesian brothers leaned against me, touched my arms, and held my hand. Oh, joy! It was a case of a cultural practice that had to be carefully negotiated.

For them it had no explicitly erotic meaning or intention, whereas for me - from highly eroticized American culture - to be touched gently made my nerves tingle and sexual ideation flood my imagination. Honouring sexual feelings, I learned, doesn't mean I need to jump into bed with every Tom, Dick or Harry – as the Solomon Islanders are wont to say.

From the outset, during my first visit in 1995, my Island brothers unconsciously helped me with their gentle physical affection, gifts of flowers, exchanges of commonplace belongings, feasting and playing together – football, volleyball, athletics. Or, more intimately, crying with me miserably as malaria shook them or me, ill for the first time away from home, and afraid.

At times, they seemed to think everything in my room was theirs to use or wear, and eventually I learned they expected me to use whatever of theirs I might need – usually their knives, as it turned out. At any time of the day or night, I might get a quiet knock on my door and a freshly broiled fish presented to me by a beaming fisherman. Give and take, laughter and tears. We bonded as brothers; these attachments have survived 21 years.

Most of the brothers from that time have left the community, some because of parental objections to life vows which in the Melanesian context require brothers to relinquish all family and tribal rights. Some simply felt called to marriage. But we still see one another when I return. So, it has been that every subsequent visit I have remembered and relived those early experiences. My life has continuity and it has been generative; I can see the difference the men in the Solomon Islands have made in my life and vice versa.

My tropical interlude all those years ago served another purpose by eventually hurling me into recovery. In recovery literature, the phenomenon of a break in a drinking habit is well documented. Without addressing the deeper issues and doing the work of consciously striving for sobriety your disease progresses during an abstinent period like a ticking time bomb deep underground. When we return to our earlier drinking habits it explodes: the experience is like going from zero to 60 miles an hour in ten seconds flat.

We didn't drink much during my first visit to the Solomons, three or four occasions are all I can remember, and they were restrained enough. I had not yet begun to think of my drinking as a problem, though I was aware of consequences that I either shrugged off or unburdened myself of in confession. Although I did not understand I was in the grip of a disease, I was trying to control myself and at the same time reward myself for periods of good behaviour – which resulted in another confession, another dry spell, another 'reward'.

After I returned from the Solomons, a brother told me I had become a bit wilder. I thought it was a compliment. Four years later, I wanted peace, not wildness.

Finally, we arrived. The truck had grunted up the rain-ravaged road, groaning over stones and man-eating ruts. I could hardly wait to go for a run. After the flower leis and green-coconut water, the welcome song and speeches, I was off.

Seeing me set off for a solo run is perhaps mildly distressing for the brothers, because one of them often materializes at my side. Solomon Islanders seem to prefer to do most things together.

With huge grins we join together, pounding along the sometimes stony, sometimes sandy road. Islanders run barefoot; they also live barefoot, their feet thickly calloused as with Vibram soles. I take a sly joy in being able to outlast some of them, though they are quick as jackrabbits in short distances, and many are natural athletes able to run great distances.

Running is often perceived to be unusual. In their traditional culture a person my age doesn't run. 'Mostly just old white peoples run, brother!' they tell me. However, plenty of young men pass me on the roads in town, and I've participated in a Fun Run with hundreds of participants in Honiara. Br Steven runs twice as far and twice as fast: he is less than half my age.

When I run alone, I'm asked if I am a soldier. Then they ask how old I am. When I say 59, they laugh and say 'Sorry!' Perhaps they think it is time to be settling down, growing a paunch.

Our neighbours are a community of Anglican religious sisters, a source of constant temptation to most of my brothers – and it's mutual. As I approach the clearing in front of the Community of the Sisters of Melanesia headquarters at Veranaaso, I hear feminine voices sing out from the canebrakes and coconut groves, 'Hello, Brother Clark!'

Fording the river, I set out around the perimeter fence of Selwyn College, a Church of Melanesia secondary boarding school. People wave and halloo. All seem to know me, and I know that reports will filter back the next day: 'I saw you running yesterday!'

Former brothers hail me and introduce their wives and children. Every time I do this run - Maravovo to Lavavasa to Paru – people hang out of the windows of passing mini-buses, or out of the back of passing flatbed trucks, and shout greetings and promises to come for a visit.

Year after year I return. Day after day I go running, subject to the weather and the beneficent universe. At times like these, the running doesn't seem hard. I understand the discipline in discipleship; it is about following your heart.

Getting out of an unbroken mental loop playing hurt and peevish messages and into heart space is a very important part of my running. It is getting into a sense of wholeness that opens me up to God's grace and healing in my life. I am surprised by different messages that bubble up as I go along. Snatches of hymns or Bible verses often occur to me, since they are the most constant source of inspiration in my life:

Trust and obey! For there's no other way
To be happy in Jesus, but to trust and obey![1]

This simple little refrain, with its camp-revival enthusiasm, is one of the gifts of the Solomon Islands and Papua New Guinea. We sing Sammis' nineteenth-century hymn frequently, and the refrain is an earworm, a relentless mosquito whine. It's become one of my running mantras. Sometimes it seems that I am simply trying to outrun the guileless words. Sometimes I mock the song, as it seems to advise giving up critical thinking. But underneath this cynical interpretation, I know that learning to trust is one of the foundational pieces of work necessary to psychological health and obedience. Radical listening to God and others is not mindless, but deeply mindful. When we listen lovingly, prayerfully, we are led into more and more mature and responsible ways of relating to God and one another. These prayers lead towards service to those in need; they give me a sense of humour and gratitude that help preserve the freedom between me and others.

Having realistic expectations of God and others facilitates trust. God is not in my delusions or off-the-mark expectations. It is important to pray for help, for cures, and transformation: miracles do happen. I stopped drinking, with God's help! Yet terrible things happen, too – and to hold God at fault for them, or delinquent in not fixing them, is not realistic. The inevitable persistence of difficulties could erode my trust in a loving God. Not to minimize devastating setbacks, but by accounting whatever persnickety aggravations that come my way simply as real life, I can then trust in meditating on God to help keep my wits about me, to dig deep for acceptance, gratitude, the moral grit I need to be honest.

In my experience, God does not prevent all problems in my life or wipe away all difficulties. But I believe the ability to deal with them is helped by God and in thinking about God. In recovery, the miracle is the removal of the desire to drink, but sobriety requires daily attention to the basic disciplines of my faith: prayer, forgiveness, letting go.

As I head east along roads crowded by looming, nattering grasses pressing like spectators against the verge, I consciously adjust my pace, to measure it for the long haul. Sometimes I run imprudently and end up gasping for air.

The village nearest the friary, Maravovo, is a long thin village, stretched along the seashore, bisected by the road. The village is like a diorama in the New York City Natural History Museum, but alive. Houses – with shaggy, sago-leaf-thatched crowns – preen like champions on their rough-cut timber plinths. I run along, absorbing the richness of village life. Pigs, chickens, dogs, cats and naked children crisscross the road in front of me. Teenage boys lounge about with head bands and tattoos; some sport dorsal cleavage.

At Maravovo village I am usually stopped by the chief, John, to welcome me and shake hands. Women, young and old, walk along balancing loads on their heads, often laundry or dishes being taken to the river to be washed. Men and women slash away at the jungle, building gardens. Others sit on their verandas, cradling children, chewing betel-nut and doubtless telling gently humorous stories, the narration of their lives.

They live most of their life outdoors, so the quotidian life is on full display. To sit around like that makes me feel slightly crazy; I struggle not to judge it as time wasted. Compulsively, I feel that I need to be productive. An aspect of my recovery is to take a Sabbath time every day, and running is part of that. Sometimes I sit around talking, or I drink a cup of tea. Trying to be still inside. Waiting on God.

Maravovo was the home of the founder of the Anglican Melanesian Brotherhood, Ini Kopuria. He was a policeman who had a vision and discerned a calling from God to found an Order in 1925. It is today the largest religious Order in the Anglican Communion, with about 500 brothers. The chief difference – apart from the size of the Order – between the Brotherhood and our community of Franciscans is that they do not take life vows, though some men stay for their whole lives. Their founding purpose was to evangelize the indigenous people of the Solomon Islands. Their work has spread to other places: Vanuatu, Papua New Guinea and the Philippines; lots of Melanesian Brotherhood Companions live in other countries.

On 6 June, the anniversary of Ini's death, the members of the Brotherhood, their Companions, and many friends join them, including the Franciscan brothers, and sisters from the other two religious orders, the Sisters of Melanesia and the Sisters of the Church. The task is to walk, singing hymns. The procession stops at regularly placed concrete crosses along the route. The brothers lead prayers in thanksgiving for Ini's life, vision and ministry, and for the furthering of his mission to share the Christian gospel with all people throughout the Islands, and indeed the world. My run follows this devotional route part way; I think the full devotional distance is 16 miles – 32 miles round trip – considerably more than I have managed so far.

Out of Maravovo I run across a series of bridges over still water, with dense, sticky-looking foliage caressing the water's surface. I've heard there are crocodiles in these parts, but I have yet to see one, to my disappointment. I once asked an old man the name of a bridge I was crossing, as he saluted my sweaty passage with an astonished smile. 'Carnivore Bridge,' he said.'Crocodiles.' I couldn't see anything. Perhaps I needed some raw meat.

At Lavavasa I pass the turn off up to St Francis School. I haven't been up there in years, but when I run in the afternoons I often meet the students leaving school. They greet me with shy smiles, the girls giggling like teenage girls anywhere. The boys shout out greetings, laughing and peppering me with questions about why I am running, where am I going so fast, where do I come from? From time to time I get spontaneous accompaniment. Once, to my astonishment, I heard feet behind me – and turned to see Cuthberta, the daughter of a former Franciscan brother, running alongside me. We ran nearly 2 miles together; from time to time she would glance at me, her eyes dancing with humour and intelligence. Her mother was once a member of the Sisters of Melanesia. Remember the constant temptation mentioned above? Her brother Clark is named after me.

When I reach Paru, my turnaround point, I stop under a spreading mango tree and savour the cool shade. I sip my tepid water. The buzzing, popping, clicking, smacking insect life thrums like my heartbeat. Primordial sounds. I stand there feeling I have reached not only a turn-around in my run, but a place where I am not in control of any of the life around me. God's own place. I can't see the insects, nor can I silence them, even if I want to. They are a constant aural presence. Their niche in this ecosystem is assured. I imagine them chewing as they make their clicking sounds. Chewing and shitting. They process the forest fibres into soil for new growth. I know from slashing gardens with the brothers that every leaf and stem hosts many of these squalling, toothy creatures. Their caterwauling casts a spell on me. I want to listen and listen. I hope to crack their code. The sounds are a sonic thread that stretches back to the earliest eons of creation. When the last proud empire collapses, provided it isn't a nuclear holocaust, the world will resound with this ovation. I love it: a spontaneous affection for all this tropical existence I don't begin to understand.

As I run back along the rutted road, I count the piglets in the undergrowth. The brothers always look amused when I point excitedly: 'There's a pig!' Some things are hard to get used to. I admire the bags of *copra* (dried coconut meat) left on the roadside, awaiting the next market truck. Copra is tremendously labour-intensive to harvest and prepare, and the financial reward is tiny. But it is a cash crop, and every penny counts in a subsistence economy.

I've helped gouge out the coconut meat from the shells and arrange it on racks over smouldering fires to dry before ramming it into voluminous burlap bags. I take great pride in doing work like that. I feel as if I've been wrestling with an angel and I want the new identity, the blessing of being a brother among these brothers. I feel it is an honour to know the basic, ancient technologies that still operate at the base of our global economy. It is hard, smelly, sweaty work.

As Gabrielle Roth has written: 'To sweat is to pray, to make an offering of your innermost self. Sweat is Holy Water, prayer beads, pearls of liquid that release your past ... sweat is an ancient and universal form of self-healing, whether done in the gym, the sauna' (Roth, *Sweat Your Prayers*, p. 17) - or, in my experience, working in the garden, or running along the road. There is dignity in this simple human life, whether it's in the work, or shaking hands with elders, or laughing with children, or testing your strength running in the heat and dust.

It has been said that the soul desires, loves and lets go, it doesn't attach or hate. When I returned from my first visit to the Solomon Islands my ego got in the way and I glommed on to the experience, as if it were a trophy to brandish – look where I went, what I did. I loved that the experience made me feel unique. I brought home bamboo flutes, palm leaf baskets, shell-inlaid carvings. I peppered my conversation with 'pijin' English phrases and stories of exotic meals.

Within a year or two brothers would flee the dinner table when I began: 'When I was in the Solomons ...' Or they'd snap: 'I don't speak pijin!' Recounting my Island experiences too often, I became a blowhard, a crashing bore, a drunk bragging. Instead of an enlarged vision of life, I had whittled it down to be all about me. These were the sobering lessons I was to learn some four miserable, bewildering years later.

Returning to the friary, I clamber up Jacob's Ladder, a flight of steps made of logs dug into the steep hillside. 'How awesome is this place!' I echo the patriarch. The 'real me' has been deeply marked by Melanesia, and I will always be grateful to God and acknowledge the debt to my community for ever sending me there.

My ministry in the Solomon Islands is not about exotic tales; rather, it is about sharing their life, helping where I can, learning all I can about life in Melanesia and, even more, learning how to be a better citizen of the world. It's about being in solidarity with them in the struggles all people have, to discover meaning and consequently our vocation, wherever we find ourselves. In Christian belief Jesus calls all of us, wherever we are, to deepen our compassion for others and ourselves. I'm called to live honestly with the gifts that I've been given as a gay man, a man in a recovery group, a preacher and teacher, and as a person committed to prayer and physical fitness as a runner – my defences against the trickster appeal of alcohol. I know that wherever I go, I have access to a great treasure in prayer and contemplation. Everywhere I go, there will be people who can show me Christ's love.

Note

1 John H. Sammis, 'Trust and Obey', 1887. Available at: <u>www.godtube.com>popular-hymns>trust-and-obey.</u>

5

Discovering kinship with all creation: Stroud, Australia

The challenge is how to begin shifting our language and ...
behaviours, our spirituality and our worship to reflect the
importance of embodiment to a sense of self, self-worth and life
in Christ. (Gooder, *Body*, p. 12)

Bursting out of the friary kitchen door, I run up the hill passing
through gum trees, orchids, banksias and other shrubs. The
driveway leads past a misty pond, a magnet for dragonflies, crowded
with water lilies, and hemmed by reeds. There had been plans to
turn this garden site into a rubbish dump before the Poor Clares and
Franciscan brothers moved there. Snatched from the jaws of that
fate, the property has become beautiful with trees and undergrowth
growing luxuriantly. Generations of brothers have propagated
native plant species: it has taken a lot of work to be natural. But
this beautiful land represents what happens when you approach the
world with a reverent, earth-honouring spirituality, a willingness to
work hard: spirit, body and mind in cahoots.

The Hermitage of St Bernardine of Siena is a simple place
located in rural Stroud, NSW, Australia. It is named after the
fifteenth-century Franciscan Vicar-General, preacher, and host
of the 'bonfires of the vanities' that occurred in response to his
preaching. He encouraged people to live simpler lives – they
burned elegant clothing, cosmetics, wigs, and high heel shoes

among other 'frivolous' things. Awkwardly, from a modern perspective, he was a man of his times: a ferocious persecutor of Jews and homosexuals – the brothers couldn't have chosen a more provocative saint. Though, to be fair, he was a peacemaker, too – ending feuds among Christians and promoting devotion to the Holy Name of Jesus.

The friary, or hermitage, is chiefly constructed of adobe mud bricks. It was built by brothers and sisters and committed lay-folk in the late 1970s – they came to call themselves 'Muddies'. The sprawling Poor Clare Monastery next door was the main project – the brothers' place is much smaller. Until they built various outbuildings and a woodframe house nearby, it was just one building with a library, chapel and five small bedrooms.

I adore the chapel. Just sitting in it, I am drawn into prayer. The rough adobe walls and the corrugated iron roof are pierced by windows scavenged from a landfill. On the wall behind the altar is a large mural of Christ Pantokrator. It's huge, much bigger than the brothers originally envisaged, but the artist/icon writer had different ideas. The chapel floor is mud, too, oiled and polished over the years to a deep glossy brown. The surface is gently uneven, like the palm of a hand. It's like a magnification of human skin, where you can see every pore and blemish, and looks like the surface of the moon.

Lifeline wrinkles crisscross the sanctuary. It is dimpled with prints of a child's bare feet mingled with the impress of an adult's boot. There is a dog's paw mark. I don't know if these marks were made intentionally or if the floor simply absorbed life during construction, and with its fossil-like markings got burnished into rough elegance. One is discouraged from wearing hard-soled shoes because it is very fragile.

Like the stone-floored caves of Assisi where St Francis prayed, which were living stone not quarried by chisel or saw, this floor of packed earth descends uninterrupted into the bowels of the earth. To walk on it barefoot, tracing the ancient patterns of the liturgy across it, feels like we are connecting with the ceremonial places of Aboriginals or the ancient threshing floors of Palestine. On the palm of God's hand.

Outside one can hear the kookaburra's bedlam call. There are scuffling, skittering sounds and a peck-peck-pecking at the roof iron. At the door, a large bed of orchids burgeons from beneath the scaly gums. Mornings, you can watch wallabies and rabbits scampering about as the brothers sing the *Benedictus*. Twice while wandering round the property I have seen koalas clinging to the trees, growling and croaking like men after an all-night bender, glaring down at me with stiff-necked annoyance. Cows from neighbouring dairy farms low and bellow. The Angelus bell is rung three times a day, reminding anybody who can hear it of the Incarnation of Our Lord. The thrill of a bell sounding has individual meaning to the hearers; bells are anointed with chrism when they are blessed, just like humans are at their baptism. They are anointed because they carry the good news, singing out the glory of God.

My running route follows the road leading up past Gunya Chiara, an adobe meeting house for large groups. The First Order Chapter met there in 2008, my first Chapter as Minister General. One of my clearest memories of that meeting is coming out in the cold August evenings and staring up at the Milky Way searing the night sky. The only other constellation I can identify in the southern hemisphere is the Southern Cross – I have seen it clearly visible above Australia, New Zealand, the Solomon Islands and Papua New Guinea. It is the giant cross on the wall of the chapel of the universe.

St Francis had a prayer he said on entering a church, a prayer that is part of the traditional devotions at the Stations of the Cross, but there's no reason it can't be said looking up at the Southern Cross in the star-bedecked heavens: 'We adore you, most holy Lord Jesus Christ, here, and in all your churches throughout all the world; and we bless you because, by your holy cross, you have redeemed the world.'

Francis loved to look at the night sky. Two and a half miles above Assisi in a steep, forested gorge on Monte Subasio, in Umbria, in the middle of Italy, is the Franciscan hermitage, the Eremo delle Carceri. There is a collection of statues there that dramatize Francis's fascination with the heavens, showing Francis, and perhaps other brothers, in various poses staring up into the sky. They are an irresistible invitation to playfulness. I have clambered on them, pretending to measure the stars with my fingers.

The sun, the moon and the stars were, of course, caught up in Francis's bear hug with life. In love with God and God's creation, Francis's love-besotted preoccupation was to find ways to point out God's love to others. God's love draws us more deeply into different ways of living in simplicity, love, joy and justice with the whole of creation, fostering kinship, which is the goalpost of Franciscan discipleship.

The Franciscan perspective is *simpatico* with that of Teilhard de Chardin, the famous French idealist philosopher and Jesuit priest, who wrote 'The Mass on the World', and prefaced his devotions:

> Since once again, Lord – though this time not in the forests of the Aisne, but in the steppes of Asia – I have neither bread, nor wine, nor altar, I will raise myself beyond these symbols, up to the pure majesty of the real itself; I, your priest, will make the whole earth my altar and on it will offer you all the labours and sufferings of the world … (*Hymn of the Universe*, cited by David Richo, Advent Quiet Day 2015, San Damiano Friary, San Francisco)

Running with Francis and Teilhard in my heart, I am reminded of the words of another soulmate. In the seventeenth century, the Anglican theologian Thomas Traherne wrote of a compelling insight as apt today as it was over 375 years ago:

> You never enjoy the world aright … till your spirit filleth the whole world, and the stars are your jewels … till you are

intimately acquainted with that shady nothing out of which the whole world was made, till you love [others] so as to desire their happiness, with a thirst equal to the zeal for your own... and more rejoice in the palace of your glory, as if it had been made but today morning. (*Centuries of Meditations*, p. xxiv)

I'll never forget priest and theologian Matthew Fox standing in front of a crowd in our outdoor chapel at Little Portion, Long Island, New York, pointing at the sky and saying: 'We're all made from stardust!' I think the cosmological perspectives of Traherne, Francis, Teilhard and Fox make clear the beauty and fragility of our fleshly existence. Everything that has been still is: we breathe the molecules of air Jesus breathed, we eat food and drink, absorbing nutrients from the earth including some part of our ancestors. It really makes people nervous when you address a crowded room with one participant hacking strenuously into a handkerchief: we are all connected, breathe in, breathe out ...

Running is a way I can strengthen the connecting bonds between me and others. Sometimes it is just wondering about the names of the roads I follow. My Australian route takes me over the crest of the hill, down the long dirt lane to the paved road. I turn right on Bucketts Way – a corruption, an Anglicization, of the original Aboriginal name. The name, sometimes spelled 'Bucketts' or 'Buckan' or 'Buckut', is derived from the Kattang language spoken by the Biripi and Worimi people, and it means 'father of stones looking down on to sacred land'. The history of the Aboriginal peoples interacting with European settlers is sad. Actually, it is tragic. God-sorrowing, damnable exploitation.

Australia is engaged in a long process of healing and reconciliation with Aboriginal peoples. Many are aiming to learn about the native perspective and experience. Aboriginal Australians trekked vast distances and kept their cosmology alive in their songs. It is part of their great gift to the world today: the notion of all creation sharing a common origin in stardust. Or that land is sacred, instead of something to own and exploit. These ideas could not be more radical or challenging. It is grieving to imagine what the 'Father of Stones' might feel as he observes the racist attacks on Aboriginal culture, attempting to erode cultural identity in a systematic way.

On February 13, 2008 Prime Minister Kevin Rudd apologized to the Aboriginal peoples and Torres Strait Islanders for the suffering inflicted on them. It was a much-needed move towards justice. Fortunately, their 40,000 year old culture has tenacious roots. Aboriginal culture is alive. The real gutsy work of healing is being done by the Aboriginal elders who preside at gatherings and tell their cultural stories, reminding people who they are. Their stories re-tell the hard-fought struggle to push back against the invasion of their land and derision of their culture. It is spiritual resilience training. Their dignity and cultural awareness are the flourishing of an ancient, hate-stopping, mind-opening heart song. Poets and performers have taken up the *cri de coeur*, expanding the cultural awareness to celebrate the full, rich humanity of their people: 'Australia, Aboriginal, Man, Human, Gay!' writes poet and actor Steven Oliver. The voices of Australia's aboriginal poets, and the dot-crazed pointillist masterpieces of their artists make plain the power of art in re-imagining spirituality and the glory of God shown in this ancient culture.

Cultural sensitivity is growing. I notice that some Australians mention the names of the indigenous peoples when they begin a talk or sermon, recognizing the original inhabitants as a step towards healing the historical wounds. I can think of only one occasion when I heard a speaker do it in the United States. I never remember to do it, which embarrasses me as I write this. It's a curious awkwardness born of shame perhaps; what stops me from mentioning the Setalcott tribe? Or the Snohomish peoples of the Lushootseed tribe? It clearly shows how deep the wounds are and the need for respect and healing between Aboriginal or First Nation or native peoples and descendants of European settlers the world over, to learn a new way of thinking about the earth and her peoples and our interconnection.

Following Bucketts Way, the scene is prosperous-looking and peaceful. Horse ranches, dairy farms, vineyards and lovely homes appear along the route. I pass by farms set on hills with grass that spreads like green fabric, patched and spliced into neatly fenced paddocks. The rich smells of the cow manure and bruised grass stems that leak milky sap bring memories that transport me home. The cattle, flushed out of ruminant complacency, scramble along the other side of the fence through the squelchy mud. Sometimes it seems as if they want to race, other times I think they are annoyed at my sudden appearance.

Every piece of coiled rope, broken fan belt, or stick on the roadside verge makes me leap out of my skin thinking of snakes. It is an added aerobic bonus. Still, all this business about snakes: I finally decide to try not to worry about them so much. I've only seen a couple of dead ones on the road, never a live one. Many people die of old age in Australia - they do not generally die from a snake bite. A little caution and respect for the creatures goes a long way towards keeping harmonious relations between the species. Herpetologists are living proof! I am a far greater hazard to snakes than they are to me. They are protected in Australia, our brothers and sisters in creation. You are not supposed to kill them: so, master your fear, lace up your boots and tread carefully. Or face a fine and/or time in prison. Among Aboriginals the Rainbow Serpent, a creator god, is one of the oldest continuing religious beliefs in the world and, if you look at Aboriginal art, still has cultural influence today.

The route is up hill and down dale. I can feel the burn in my legs as I run. Once after a long flight and several days of enforced inactivity, I came to the top of a hill along this route. Bent over, gasping, trembling a bit, I was unaware a man had stopped his car and got out. I looked up as he called out to me: 'G'day mate! Yer allright?!' At first, I was confounded, then deeply touched. This was the first time anybody had ever stopped for me. I took a deep breath: 'Just out of shape, but okay, thanks!' I hollered back. 'No worries,' he said with a smile. 'Take care now.'

Whether I am in top shape or not, there have been times when I 'hit the wall', from dehydration or not eating enough beforehand, especially on long runs. Bent over and breathing hard, I debate whether to give up or press on. This debate is familiar to me in many areas of my life: friendships, writing projects, community administration, and my vocation not least of all. I suspect it is a debate many religious, as well as others, have. Perhaps this is why 'Persevere' was the message on my plain dark-brown profession cake in 1993. I felt somewhat nonplussed when I first saw it, expecting 'Congratulations!' wreathed with roses. But this will be my funeral cake, I suspect.

Perseverance is a choice and a grace. When I am doubled over breathing heavily, my legs aquiver, sweat sheeting down my face and back, I am praying furiously: Help me, help me, Lord. At that moment, common sense would seem to counsel stopping, but I also know that if I keep going it will get better. My body will adjust and the burn in the muscles will go away. Sometimes the best moments of running – and life and ministry – come after having moved through a moment when I was convinced I couldn't go on.

Perseverance is one of those recurring themes I think and pray about as I run – and it brings back memories. Once I was sitting in my room at Little Portion eating ice cream. When you want to drink, I was told, eat sweets. Cradling half a gallon of ice cream, I was eating miserably when Brother Jon stuck his head in my room.

'What're you doing?' Swollen with self-pity and self-loathing, I shot back: 'What the hell does it look like I'm doing? I hate my life, I hate this house, and I hate you!' And I threw the ice cream at him. 'Hey!' he said, catching it. Then he came into the room, over to me.

'Stand up!' he said. I stood, ready for a fight. But he put his hands on my shoulders: 'I know this is a very difficult time for you. But I promise you, one day you will count your sobriety as the very best thing in your life.' Then he gave me a hug, encouragement to persevere on the road to freedom. Thank God for people who loved me when I couldn't love myself, or I'm sure I'd have given up religious life and sobriety before now.

In sobriety, on the one hand we talk about perseverance as doing the next right thing, of asking for help in times of temptation and distress, of keeping ourselves spiritually fit with daily prayer and meditation. In other words, we must put some effort into staying sober. On the other hand, we say the only way forward is to let go, to acknowledge our powerlessness over alcohol, and relinquish any fantasy of controlling other people or situations that we find ourselves in.

Most of us cannot find sobriety through fiat or pure willpower. The only willpower required is a daily turning of the will over to God. Applying effort and letting go seem like opposites. But taken together the torque is just right, shown repeatedly to twist the brain into a new way of perceiving.

I keep a copy of an address to some men about to be ordained Jesuit priests that a friend sent me, in which a priest asks the men: 'Are you weak enough?'[1] Life and ministry and vocation are not about powering through situations, but about relying on God and my community in prayer.

I remember when I told Br Justus, our Minister Provincial at the time, that I had gone into recovery for alcoholism. We were standing on a broken sidewalk strewn with litter in Bushwick, Brooklyn: a fitting place for an admission of brokenness and failure. I couldn't meet his eyes; shame made me look at the ground. 'So,' I said, summing up my confession, 'if you want me to, I will leave the Order. I have brought shame on it. I am so very, very sorry.' I knew with certainty that he would regretfully agree, and I'd be dismissed to slink away.

Finally, after a pause long enough to make me look up at him, I saw tears in his eyes, and he said, 'Now you are truly one of us! We are all broken men seeking God's healing and love in the company of each other. I love you,' he said, giving me a warm hug, making curious clucking sounds like a hen protecting her chick.

God's grace and power is made perfect in human weakness. This does not mean I should go and get drunk. Rather, when faced with the temptation to give up, to throw in the towel because of shame, fear or feeling inadequate, I need to entrust myself entirely to God. I ask for help from God, and my brothers, and then wait for the renewed perspective that comes when I let go of the desire to escape my feelings or chemically change them. Drinking, of course, offers the beguiling alternative that I deserve a little reward, some peace of mind, to 'take the edge off' – but the rewards are more reliably found in gentle breathing, or a slow jog through the late afternoon.

Spiritually, there have been many moments when I have felt knocked down, ready to give up. I think of the deaths of beloved brothers and sisters. Or the times when religious life seemed trivial and not worth the effort to sustain it. In some provinces of the Order, we are a small group of ageing men, so diverse that our interests are sometimes in direct opposition and I feel isolated and foolish. Who cares about religious life? It's not worth the irritation, I whine to myself. The best piece of advice I ever received about these demoralizing moods that so often result from judging my brothers is to pray for them, asking that they be blessed with every good thing that I want for myself: peace, joy, love, a meaningful life. At first, I objected that this was just asking too much, but was sternly advised to take a moment every single day for at least two weeks to pray for whomever I was finding problematic.

When I have been faithful in this practice, I have never been disappointed. Hate, not to say pique, dissolved into acceptance and a species of love. What more could I ask? I could be the person I want people to believe I am.

I turn around at the bridge over Mammy Johnsons River in Stroud Road. I always look for the sign. We used to call my grandmother 'Mammy', a custom started by a young neighbour of my grandparents when my mother was a child. Thinking about my beloved fudge-making Mammy, her whacky high-spirited take on life, lifts my spirits. Most of the stories we tell about her are funny ones, endearing memories of her nearly 100 years of life. She and my grandfather – who was also known as 'Pops' – were married for over 75 years: talk about perseverance. My mother often marvelled that their marriage seemed to deepen after the 50th Golden Wedding Anniversary. Sometimes the best comes late in life: it's a gamble, and a great blessing – but not worth counting on. We only have today – that's why I run. The enjoyment factor of my physical wellbeing, my mental state and my spiritual condition mount higher and higher as I open myself to the world, and running is one of the ways I do that for now.

The endorphin rush of exercise is the body's natural high, a convincing glimpse of the possibilities of life without drugs or alcohol: a 'pledge of the hope of our calling' as we say in the liturgy, describing the joy of the saints. Wishing for a better, happier life does not actually achieve it. When I started acknowledging my body's claims on my attention, I discovered a host of connections with the people around me and those who have gone before me.

Science and mysticism make the connection between our bodies and the world around us. Taking my place among those who love beauty, hate oppression and violence, I realized that I take care of myself with exercise, nutrition and prayer because Jesus calls us to it in his teachings. Taking care of your health might be a small thing but, as Jesus points out, if you are faithful in small things, you will be entrusted with greater ones.

Attention to nutrition and exercise can lead to a deeper sense of self-worth, attention to the earth, the health of peoples and all creatures, everywhere. Running back up the dirt track to the friary I count wallabies, once I counted five. These extraordinary kangaroo-looking creatures with their offspring in their pouches graze on the grass, watching me closely. They live somewhere among the trees, I guess. The woodland area is their home, too. 'G'day mates!' I call out to them. As I trot past them to the house, they leap into thickets and around tree trunks. I envy their grace and speed over the tricky terrain. A deep spiritual significance resonates in my heart. Not least because we are outside, creatures on the hoof running around, we are related.

Note

1 The Revd Michael Buckley, 'The Wisdom of Rev. Michael J. Buckley, S.J.: The Downward Path'. Available at: www.servant-leaderassociates. com/Servant-Leader_Associates/Faith_Perspectives_files/The%20 Wisdom%20of%20Rev%20Michael%20J%20Buckley.pdf(accessed 22.11.16).

6

Joining the spiritual and physical together in Franciscan spirituality: Assisi, Italy

> In the minds of many, 'spiritual' is the opposite of 'physical'; the 'spiritual' is associated with God and the 'physical' is associated with the earth; the 'spiritual' with all things good and the 'physical' with all things bad … This attitude manifests itself as a general uncertainty about a Christian attitude to anything that falls under the heading of 'physical'. An interesting example of this might be attitudes towards the environment. (Gooder, *Body*, p. 4)

Assisi gleams on the craggy, tree-clad flanks of Mount Subasio. The fields, vineyards and orchards climb up from the valley floor to the walls of the ancient city. Bells sing out glory and praise, calling people to prayer. Perhaps the greatest architectural differences since the time of Francis are two basilicas bookending the town, one built in his honour, and the one for Clare at the opposite end. The church for Francis was built over an area that was previously a rubbish dump. The city is now a World Heritage site. The stone buildings are caparisoned with geraniums in season.

Through open doors, shop fronts extrude racks of religious bangles on to the streets like overripe figs fallen to the ground, spilling their guts. Escher-esque staircases wriggle beneath houses and skitter up the hillsides, trees take root in the cracks of walls. The buildings and the medieval urban environment are jewels that catch the eye and coax people to linger in the tiny town. Artists are partly responsible for consolidating Assisi's stature. Among others, Giotto's famous cycle of frescoes in the Basilica of St Francis explicitly make the parallels between Francis and the Christ he loved and served: a riotous celebration of colour, symbolic of a passionate spiritual relationship. The city is filled with art and spiritual significance for people all over the world, because Francis said his faithful 'yes' to God. He danced and sang on the margins of the world to call it home to sanity.

In February 2015, I lived in Assisi, to serve as chaplain to an English-speaking, mostly Anglican, congregation that meets there. I lived on the Via San Gabriele dell'Addolorata, just up from Piazza del Comune, in an apartment belonging to the Society of St Francis. Some days snow swirled down on the narrow medieval streets, bells thudded heavily, and brown muffled friars shuffled by, their muttered *pace e bene* barely audible through their scarves. But more often, the sun blazed out brightly, frost sparkled in the lee of the buildings. The potted cyclamens on doorsteps and in windowboxes flared up red with hot-blooded bravura. In the afternoons, I liked to open the large glass door on to the balcony to let the sun and fresh air fill the apartment. Best of all, however, was pulling on a windbreaker and dashing out of the door for a run to Santa Maria degli Angeli and Portiuncula.

I crossed the Piazza del Comune where people snapped photos by the fountain, and posed in front of the Temple of Minerva, even in winter. I wove through groups of people clumping up like hungry sparrows in front of the little coffee shop next to the Town Hall, then leaped down a very steep hill along Via Portica to Via Arnaldo Fortini which leads into Via San Francesco. It was like flying; I fantasized I was an Olympic runner skimming over obstacles, with the words of Eric Liddell from *Chariots of Fire* repeating in my brain: 'To run and feel the Lord's pleasure!' (Hugh Hudson, *Chariots of Fire*, 1981. Story by Colin Welland.) Indeed.

There is a great fresco of Francis in a flying chariot in the upper basilica, recalling Elijah zooming up to heaven in a fiery chariot. The obvious comparison shows Francis as a prophet. Afire with enthusiasm, I ran straight on to the Basilica of St Francis, then headed towards the lower basilica and the great Piazza Inferiore di San Francesco. Running often gives me tastes of euphoria. Running through Assisi was twice the good feeling because I felt I was at play in the home of my spiritual ancestor.

I ran out of Porta San Francesco and down to the head of the stairs that lead to the Via San Francesco. This brick path leads directly to the great church of St Mary of the Angels. The path was built after the 1996 earthquake that rocked Assisi. People from all over the world made donations to rebuild Assisi, but principally from Italy, it appears, from the names of their home towns. Each contribution was acknowledged with a brick. These were inscribed with their names and cities and laid in a path. In 1999, I bought a brick for a dear friend from Tacoma. In 2015, I scanned the bricks as I ran, looking for his name. I couldn't find it. If I'd kept the certificate I was given when I bought it (and where would a small piece of paper be 16 years and several moves later?) I could have tracked his brick on the internet. I guessed his brick is probably one of the ones that is worn smooth, only a few discernible letters surviving, or missing from where they had to dig up the path to lay a pipe or underground wiring.

Like the characters in the *Wizard of Oz* skipping along the yellow brick road, I ran along the brick path to St Mary of the Angels and the Little Portion, singing, brooding, fearful, happy – different days, different memories, different emotions.

Emerging from the shady flanks of Mount Subasio, the path crosses an area that my guide book says might be the place Francis encountered the leper. It's still a wooded area, though more a copse than a forest. And it looks nothing like Zeffirelli's film with the extraordinary waterfall (Zeffirelli, *Brother Sun, Sister Moon*, 1972). No waterfall. Vespas and Fiats whizzing by notwithstanding, it is easy to imagine Francis riding through the area, his horse disconsolately scuffling the ground, Francis absorbed with angst: 'What am I supposed to do with my life?'

Then suddenly he encounters the one thing he is most afraid of; ghosts and goblins have nothing on a person rotting away with voracious sores gnawing their features. In Francis's time these unfortunate lepers wore clackers around their necks to warn people off. In addition, they were given a funeral prior to their death – which they were forced to attend – and then they were driven out to the forest to die over time, the fearful community's obligations to them fulfilled. They were, in many ways, the walking dead. As I remember and understand it from my novitiate, they survived on charity; compassionate people took food to them or left it for them to find.

Part of the miracle in Francis's meeting with the leper is that for once he did not clamp his nose with a scented cloth or turn and ride away as quickly as possible. By a passionate impulse of the Holy Spirit, he was propelled into the place of grace; he leaped from his horse with a courtly gesture. Then, more astonishingly, he kissed the leper – at least according to some chroniclers. I like to think it could have been this way, because I am always attracted by reckless love. He embraced what he feared the most, finding in the action the reward to all who 'come out' that at last he was free to be most fully himself. Years later, at the end of his life, when he was writing his *Testament*, Francis said: 'for when I was in sin, it seemed too bitter for me to see lepers. And the Lord himself led me among them and I showed mercy to them. And when I left them, what had seemed bitter to me was turned into sweetness of soul and body. And afterwards I delayed a little and left the world' (St Francis, 'The Testament', in Armstrong, Hellmann and Short, *Francis of Assisi* vol. 1, p. 124).

This story of Francis and the leper reminds me of an early experience of my own, going as a callow seminarian in 1981 to volunteer for one day at the Catholic Worker on the Lower East

Side of Manhattan. Three of us went there to help the Workers prepare and serve a meal. I was more than a little alarmed by the homeless people who crowded around the doorway. My heart was hammering painfully by the time we got into the building.

When the man asked what skills I had to offer, I volunteered to cook. My memory has been coloured by telling the story repeatedly. I always say I made a soup of carrots, wieners and milk. Whatever went into that pot, I was repulsed by it.

After serving it to all the guests, I was told to take a bowl of it and sit at a spare place among the homeless people. Intellectually, I recognized the aptness of this move, but never have I wanted to be somewhere else more desperately. But I sat and spooned the goop into my mouth while trying to hold my breath – a childhood trick learned when eating pea soup, to try not to taste it.

'Hey!' I heard from across the table. I ignored the voice. 'Hey, white boy!' Glancing up I could see I was being addressed. 'What'cha doin' here?' a man asked. I told him, primly, about being a seminarian and coming to experience urban ministry. Since he started the questions I reciprocated, hesitantly, not wanting to offend or condescend though my scruples were probably condescending enough. 'What are *you* doing here?'

So, we started to talk. He introduced me to others sitting next to him. My fear dropped away a little. Though I remained woodenly self-conscious, I began to feel the rightness of things, sharing a bowl of soup with these men. No kisses, but I felt a glimmer of recognition, a promise of being at home among displaced peoples. Years later, I told a man writing about the spirituality of gay men that I was attracted to work with the poor and homeless – because I felt homeless, too. Like the Lion, Tin Man and Scarecrow in the *Wizard of Oz*, my sense of differentness finally had a creative purpose.

Out of these evocative woods, the stretch across the valley is dead flat. I loved picking up my pace. Francis and his brothers walked this way over and over, probably barefoot. Once I brought some brothers from the Solomon Islands and Papua New Guinea to Assisi before we all went to be chaplains at the Lambeth Conference in Canterbury, England, and they wanted to do everything just as Francis had done it, usually preferring to walk places.

In the film *Brother Sun, Sister Moon*, the Spoleto Valley is portrayed as a poppy-speckled wonder, and Francis and his brothers run through it barefoot, singing. So that's what we did – though we wore shoes. That film, for good or ill, is the primary source from which my Franciscan brothers in the Solomon Islands and Papua New Guinea are introduced to the message of St Francis and how they share it with their neighbours. It is the governing image most of the brothers there have of Assisi.

We walked and ran all over the city and its environs. When they saw a pretty girl they would call out, shyly, *sotto voce*: 'Clare! Clare!' Nobody except us understood what they were saying and why. It was all great fun. But the running became a way for us to connect with Francis; now it is a kind of prayer in which I am running with Francis, to Francis, and sometimes away from Francis, on my bad days.

Without St Francis and St Clare and Franciscan spirituality, Assisi is only a town like many others in Italy. The Franciscans put it on the map, as the brick-laid path with the names of so many devoted people evoking a great cloud of witnesses makes abundantly clear. Over time it has become an ensign, a sign marking a place of peace. Like petrol on a fire, the genius of Francis flared up in the first minutes of the thirteenth century and hasn't gone out. His gift to the world was, in part, about perceiving the work of God in all things, the evidence of the spiritual among the shimmering nebulae, and the light-charged matter of the universe.

He could pick out the indelible, uniquely patterned, give-away fingerprints in nature that led him back to the Maker. He looked at trees and streams, stared into the fire, and sniffed the breeze. He saw the many shades of green, the colour of the Spirit, in the treetops. The leafy canopy's restless play semaphored a message to surrender to the rhythms of redeeming grace. Purling streams splashing over stones, welling up from hidden sources in the stony mountains, murmured a song of cleansing, of baptism. In the fire, he saw the red-hot glow of light and heat that brightens the night – brother to the Light that can shine into every heart. Fire can soften the hardest metals, and spiritual fire fed by the wood of the cross can soften iron wills, so on the anvil of grace they may yield to the hammer blows of conscience.

The red-hued glow from the heart of the embers is only a pale imitation of the blinding light of the sun. The sun is the emblem of the Son reigning over heaven and earth. The moon Francis claimed as his sister: the shy waxing and waning orb shedding its chaste glow on his night-time dreams, a beautiful face peering at him as he sang below in the moonlight, perhaps just like the radiant, loving look of Clare. The wind, cleansing, singing, whispering the message of God to seek out the least, the lost and the lonely and, in doing so, find the Lord of glory.

The world touched the imagination of Francis, opened his eyes to the rightful place of everything in God's creation, himself included. This sober perspective he called penance. The life of penance is at the heart of Franciscan life. For him it was not enough to make a confession, a ritual act, kneeling in hard places to speak the barely speakable. Penance is about going in a different direction, swimming against the cultural currents and refusing the blandishments of money and comfort and power, because these things lead ineluctably to the will to protect them and war to secure them.

The two qualities he sought to cultivate in himself and impress on his followers as necessary to the gospel life – minority and poverty – were the qualities that expressed penance. Living differently meant giving up power, status and ego-strokes. He called this minority. If you seriously take up that calling, then you need to give up things – to embrace poverty.

Aware of his own frailty, Francis drew moral lessons from calamity and hardship: it is because of your sins – or 'my' sins, as he often said – the Lord has caused this to happen. He used every occasion to draw the attention of men and women to God, to hear God's call to live differently on the earth, repenting of violence, war, exploitation, rooting out the source of these sins where they lurk in the human heart as pride, lust, fear and greed.

In my own flailing efforts to live this Franciscan minority and poverty, I refuse to use airmiles for upgrades, choosing to sit without perks or 'benefits', deaf to the pandering spiel of airlines about luxury and the feel-good ranks of platinum, gold, silver, what have you. Airmiles get used for unplanned, necessary trips. I have had many arguments with people about this. If I must fly, I want to be like the poorest student on the flight; they say I am crazy. I say: mission accomplished!

For me it was the hint of madness in the joy that partly attracted me to the example of Francis; we all need a bit of madness. 'Pazzo! Pazzo! Crazy, crazy!' the townspeople called after him – as Francis, this once-delicate young man, son of a wealthy merchant, begged for stones for his building projects, and food to eat. He did other crazy things too, rolling in pig shit when initially thrown out of the Vatican, building a family from snow, turning and turning until he fell down to choose the way he should go along the road, emphasizing his total dependence on God. Later his 'craziness' shamed the naysayers and touched many hearts longing to be free.

Maybe I flatter myself when I say it was Franciscan craziness when I decided I wanted out from a future I could only see as predictable and establishmentarian as an Episcopal priest. To run barefoot through the fields. To live a life of prayer such as that which provoked the forays of Francis into the enemy Sultan's territory.

It sounded thrilling and a way of transforming my life. But I didn't yet have the self-awareness to tease out the strands of my immature neediness and compulsiveness, from the authentic gospel freedom of Francis. I had a steep learning curve ahead of me. But, as Brother Derek of my community once said to me, as I fretted over the ambiguity of my early motives: 'God uses whatever we give him.' God took the impetuousness of Francis and his real love and made something happen that has had a permanent impact on Christianity and beyond.

Francis raised up the strands of humility, love and joy in Christian thought and devotion and made them shimmer with intensity and joy. The impact of Francis is evidenced in the lives of many people who think highly of Francis, honour him, yet do not feel any need to take on the whole credal burden of Catholic Christianity.

The other great saint from Assisi is Clare. Calling herself 'the little plant of St Francis', she sank her roots in his worldview and grew to be a sequoia in her own right. Her Franciscan life started with a run, too. She shoved her way out of the 'door of the dead' at the base of her family's home in Assisi one Palm Sunday evening, and ran off to rendezvous with Francis and his brothers in the woods below the walls of Assisi. Her breakout on that night was clearly a signal of her desire to follow the crucified Christ, and it was her avowed death to the privilege and power of her aristocratic family.

Enraged, they chased after her, but by the time they caught up with her, her hair had been cut off, and she had received a habit from Francis. This urgent dash for freedom and break with her family must have been incredibly painful as well as exhilarating. It is a testimony to her character and evidence of God's hand in it all that her sister and mother and some other female relatives eventually came to join her.

After a short time living in other religious houses, Francis gave Clare and her fledgling community San Damiano. There, she lived without belligerence and bellicosity or any of the soul-destroying presumptions of a well-born woman who may even sweetly instruct her maid to do the laundry, the cooking and the sweeping up.

Calling herself a servant, she was radically egalitarian. She was inspired by minority and poverty, recognizing in these things the way to spiritual freedom. In the words of a later blessed one, Brother Lawrence, she did everything, no matter how menial, to the glory of God without an attitude of condescension.

In interviews after her death, before she was canonized as a saint, the sisters spoke of great grace in the way she bore her poverty and whatever hardships it entailed: 'she was never seen disturbed … and she was always rejoicing in the Lord' (Armstrong, *Clare of Assisi*, p. 156). If you are going to take a vow of poverty, that is the best way to do it.

Clare, like most 'poor' religious, had to choose between accepting privileges thrust upon her in honour of her commitment, and rejecting all efforts by others to cheapen the currency of her poverty. The watchfulness Clare needed, not to compromise for herself and her sisters the 'privilege of poverty', is soberly brought to mind whenever I hear the seductive, gratified stories among religious that some pious person 'recognized the significance of the habit' and gave them an upgrade in travel or accommodation, or helped a brother jump a queue. Her wisdom is brought to mind even more during circular discussions about what to do with a large bequest to the Order – should we keep it, give it away, or use it for special projects? The Church of Clare's day was exceedingly apprehensive of allowing her to live without lands and property – to live without financial security. But as pilgrims and strangers in the world, she actively sought for herself and her sisters the roller-coaster of living supported by alms. Unfailingly polite, after an exchange of courtly worded letters, she finally wore down the cardinals and received from the Pope approval of her 'way of life' – one that included absolute poverty.

What was at stake for her in this? Perhaps, most simply, it was the longing to be free – to follow the example of Christ in his poverty and to signal the utter defencelessness and vulnerability of God who sent his Son to live and die as one of us. Money entails obligations – gratitude, sympathy, co-optation. Does this bug you? It bugs me. Clare, I am sure, would smile. Also, there was a bracing desire for self-determination. Her Rule was the first Rule for religious women in the Western Church written by a woman – or, perhaps more accurately, women: 'Clare was an innovator, creating a new form of religious life, not only *for* but also more especially *with* her sisters. All of them, inspired by Clare's vision, took an active part in creating the life they shared' (Julien, 'Clare's Model of Leadership', p. 184).

The Church hasn't always recognized or appreciated the perspectives and gifts of women. I remember when in the 1960s and early 1970s my sisters weren't allowed to be acolytes, and there is the painful furore that still rages around the global Church over the ordination of women, though there are places where they serve as equal to men, even as bishops.

Tenacious as a limpet, Clare stuck to her convictions arrived at through prayer and community discernment. She was buried with the papal bull confirming her Rule.

Clare is celebrated for a spectacular event that she never refers to, fittingly enough. The legend of her life describes how she delivered Assisi from the Saracens (Armstrong, *Clare of Assisi*, p. 300). In 1230, on a Friday in September, hearing of a tatterdemalion band closing in on the walls of Assisi, she reportedly took up the Blessed Sacrament and went to stand in view of the marauders. Like poking a flower in the barrel of a gun or standing in the way of a tank hellbent on destruction or holding a placard of a beloved child 'disappeared' by tyrannical power, the witness of Clare was simple, wordless – empowered by faith and inspired by the Spirit to shame the strong and foil their deadly arrogance.

Did she know the men would turn back? Did he know the tank wouldn't run him over, adding to the carnage of Tiananmen Square? Did they know the Argentinian dictator wouldn't arrest and torture them too? I don't think so. What is it about a defenceless person who refuses to run scared?

It challenges the assumptions of oppressors; it stymies the fierceness of soldiers. Certainly, the not-insignificant detail that Clare held the Blessed Sacrament speaks to Christians of God's never-failing presence with the poor, the weak, the orphans and defenceless. With God, all things are possible.

Clare and Francis emerged at a critical time in history. The tweets and blatts of arrogant, trumping political combatants, snickering in their overweening pride and nepotistic machinations for power, involved the people of Assisi – and people in the Middle Ages in general – in war after war. To answer every idiocy with a counter statement was impossible and would mean the terms of the controversy were being set by the aggressor. Instead, by the way they lived, these holy people held up, in Clare's own term, 'a mirror' (Armstrong, *Clare of Assisi*, p. 55) to their times, and in that flash of reflection people saw the Truth and how far they'd fallen from it.

Recognizing that they were created in the image of God, Franciscans and Poor Clares were moved to godly repentance and inspired to live radically differently from their surrounding culture. For instance, it was forbidden for the members of the Franciscan Third Order to bear arms (Cardinal Hugolino, 'Memoriale Propositi', in Meersseman OP, *Dossier de L'Ordre de la Pénitence*, p. 101), although it has been noted that, despite refusing to fight for the defence of their city or lords, they did not neglect their other civic responsibilities. Thousands of men and women flocked to Francis's First and Third Orders, and Clare was soon establishing convents near and far.

The appeal of the life of Francis and Clare has cut across class and gender lines for generations. From the very beginning, people who were married also longed to be part of this movement of the Spirit. With a flourish of intellectual suppleness that is astonishing in any period or age, especially by a religious, Francis blessed them and established the Third Order – married or single people living in their own homes without a promise of celibacy. Following Francis is a wide-open road in terms of the form of life: it simply depends on whatever call is given.

Theory is easy to expound. The vision of Francis was capacious. A highway to God. But religious life can feel like a crumbly little goat path on a sheer cliff face as one tries to live simply, chaste in body and mind, resisting violence in thought, word and deed, and living consciously and attentively to the rest of creation. The tricky terrain adds to the thrill. I can see where I want to be and am happy to have found this hardscrabble route: a life of prayer, service, community with my brothers and sisters, and enough laughter to keep me going forward.

Often, as I pressed across the Spoleto Valley, breathing in the cool winter air in 2015, thoughts and prayers about the early Franciscan movement filled my mind. The transformation of Francis's and Clare's lives has inspired many to try to live as they did, and I am one of them. When I first broached the idea of a vocation to religious life, I was visiting my parents for dinner during the time I was living and working in Tacoma. At the end of dinner, I nervously began, 'I have something I want to talk with you about.' My parents looked at me eagerly. 'I've been thinking and praying about my life,' I said, 'and I think I want, I feel called, to be a friar.' It was not what they expected to hear from their 30-year-old son. 'Is that some kind of a monk?' my mother asked. The conversation careened this way and that. Assumptions and hopes and fears long unspoken came tumbling out like mice from beneath the grain bins, and I left the house that evening deeply shaken, wondering what was going to happen next.

I remembered St Francis's naked caper in Assisi after being sued by his father to return money he'd taken to rebuild the church of San Damiano. It precipitated a break with his family and shoved him into the arms of Christ: 'I no longer have a father here on earth, but only my Father who art in heaven.'

My parents and I danced the steps pioneered by Francis and

his parents, the Bernadones, long ago in Assisi. My idealism, their dashed hopes, led to misunderstandings and quite a bit of pain. But the dance ended happily for me and my family. With a flourish of grace, at Christmas dinner in 1988, my mother proposed a toast after Dad's prayer before the meal: 'To our Lord Jesus Christ whose birth we celebrate, to St Francis who loved him, and to Clark who loves them both.'

The lives and examples of Francis and Clare, and those of a huge number of religious people through the ages, have given me a way to name my spiritual experience and to open my heart to God. Ideas inspired by meditation on the life and example of Francis have been liberating. A sign of spiritual progress is, as Bruce Springsteen suggests, 'to do all the unimportant things well … It ain't what you're doing, but what happens while you're doing it that counts' (Springsteen, *Born to Run*, p. 453).

Everything I do is part of my spiritual life, mundane chores are spiritual discipline, everyday objects can draw me into the presence and activity of the Divine in the world. It becomes possible to believe that goodness can triumph over evil – and, also, that forgiveness and simplicity can distinguish the lives of men and women: it's not pie in the sky.

I am grateful that I have been able to make several visits to Assisi. My first visit in May 1999 was a gift in celebration of my Profession of Life Vows. But I must honestly confess that I travelled to Assisi one month before I quit drinking, and it was frankly an indication that vocation can inhabit our hearts, side by side with spiritual blindness and denial. My idealism, love, calling was all true, and I longed for my life to be transformed by God, but I had no sense that I had an addiction, an illness, a compulsion that made me thirsty, twisted my judgement under the influence of the alcohol, and dragged my sorry backside into some dark places.

My journal from that time is an account of a man writhing in the grip of an addiction: I could not rid myself of my troubles by my willpower alone. My mind was always making allowances, giving me permission that friends in sobriety later recognized and lovingly challenged. I couldn't name alcoholism yet, but over and over in that journal appear admonitions to myself: 'I must not drink that much again.' A few entries later, a confession that perhaps I had had too much to drink. When I wasn't berating myself, I was extolling the taste and abundance of the wine and brandy and beer and everything else I found to drink. Harder to write about then – and now – were the corollary traumas of binge drinking: hookups, blackouts and shame.

How could I tell people what I really did during that visit? I limped away thinking I never would. It had been a disaster. But just six weeks later, I was talking to a man who was to become my sponsor in recovery. He is a Franciscan too, and he asked me: 'When you were at the tomb in the basilica of St Francis, did you pray the prayer they have there for conversion of life?' Indeed, I had. Also, I had prayed something very eloquent, like 'Oh my God, help me please!'

My friend paused, then smiled at me, 'And now your prayer has been answered.'

I started to complain, 'Yes, but I never thought …' The thought of living without alcohol in my life was overwhelming. How would I ever have fun again?

'Perhaps you need to re-define fun,' he said. Was throwing up fun? Lying, was that fun? Stealing from the brothers? At this last I started to protest that I never stole. But, he said, did you tell them you were going to drink with the money? What did you tell them?

I said, of course I didn't tell them that. I guess I sometimes said I was going to buy food or have a meal out. 'Right,' he said, cutting me off. 'You lied and stole.'

This crossroads of faith and sobriety with my evasive, compulsive behaviours translated for me into a terse: 'Grow up!' As Eugene Peterson writes: 'Becoming mature means refusing to live a reduced life, refusing a minimalist spirituality … [and yet] becoming mature takes a long time, with many rest stops along the way; it cannot be hurried. Becoming mature is a complex process that defies simplification; there are no short cuts' (Peterson, *Practice Resurrection*, p. 175).

Sobriety is a spiritual way of life for me. Once I had a name for what ailed me, and friends who could talk about it with me, I began to become more and more reliant on God, the only way to find the maturity I needed.

Literature teaching about recovery from alcoholism and Franciscan spiritual writings have a shared text. The Prayer Attributed to St Francis, 'Lord, make me an instrument of your peace', is the centrepiece of some teachings in recovery about meditation and prayer. The first time I heard this prayer read in a recovery meeting, I was deeply embarrassed. It was as if my mother had come into the room; I did not want the different parts of my life to touch in such an intimate way. But division and separation, secrets and shame are the drinker's game. Integration, wholeness and openness is the sober strategy.

When I got over my shame attack, I saw my fault in never taking what I learned as a novice about meditation seriously enough. It was to me something religious people did but I found it to be like sitting on a large pebble – very uncomfortable – and hard not to stray into fantasies.

Encountering it in sobriety, I suddenly understood that here was the life-or-death choice. Meditation and prayer were the only things that could keep me sober, because only God could fill the crazy longing that I had for years tried to fill with booze. To my astonishment, what I longed for *was* God.

Reaching the Basilica di Santa Maria degli Angeli, I rested for a moment on a bench outside. Embedded in the bigger church is the tiny ninth-century Church of St Mary of the Angels called Portiuncula – or the Little Portion. It was named because it was on a little portion of land given to Francis by some Benedictine monks. It looks a bit peculiar to have a small, highly decorated chapel in the middle of an enormous marble-floored church. But it is obviously a holy place.

I appreciate the forbearance and goodwill of the brothers managing the crowds of pilgrims and tired tourists with humour and graciousness, trying to preserve a sense of holiness and prayer amid the diverse people, many of whom want to capture the moment with cameras and cell phones, snapping themselves in a selfie: 'I was here!' It is one of the churches re-built by Francis in the first flush of his enthusiasm to 'rebuild the Lord's house'. This was before, as he said, the Lord gave him brothers and showed him what he was to do next.

That shift from construction crew to evangelists took Francis and his brothers some time to manage. Because of criticism of his band of brothers and their life together, he walked to Rome in order to ask the Pope to approve his gospel way of life. At issue was the similarity between the early Franciscans and other groups of that day committed to poverty, who preached against the Church's wealth, many of whom won for themselves the status of heretics in the Church's eyes. Francis did not want to be a heretic. He had a remarkable encounter with the Pope. Both men, after all, took direction from dreams. The Pope dreamed of a small man holding up a church that was falling down and realized he was called by the Spirit to help Francis and to give approval to his simple way of life. Francis had a dream too; perhaps it was a meditative reverie, but it is extraordinary in its imagery.

It is told in 'The Legend of the Three Companions':

Once God's saint had prayed [that God would reveal his will to him] as the Lord Pope suggested, the Lord spoke figuratively to him in spirit, 'There was a little, poor and beautiful woman in a desert, whose beauty fascinated a great king. He wanted to take her as his wife, because he thought that, from her, he would have handsome sons. After the marriage was celebrated and consummated, there were many sons born and raised. Their mother spoke to them in this way, "My sons, do not be ashamed, for you are sons of the king. Therefore, go to his court and he will provide for all your needs." When they went to see the king, he was struck by their good looks, and noticing a resemblance to himself in them, he asked them, "Whose sons are you?" When they answered that they were the sons of the little poor woman living in the desert, the king embraced them with great joy. "Do not be afraid," he said, "for you are my sons. If strangers are fed at my table, how much more will you, who are my lawful sons." He then ordered the woman to send to his court all of the children she had borne to be fed.'

When these things had been shown to blessed Francis while he was praying, the man of God understood that the poor woman signified him. After he completed his prayer, he presented himself to the Supreme Pontiff and narrated point-by-point the story that the Lord had revealed to him. 'My Lord,' he said, 'I am that poor little woman whom the loving Lord, in his mercy, has adorned, and through whom he has been pleased to give birth to legitimate sons. The King of kings has told me that he will nourish all the sons borne to me, because, if he feeds strangers, he must provide for his own. For if God gives temporal goods to sinful men out of love for providing for his children, how much more will he give to Gospel men who deserve these things out of merit.'

(Armstrong, Hellmann and Short, *Francis of Assisi*, vol. 2, p. 97)

This Promethean vision, gender-bending and startling, indicates the generative, life-giving spirituality of Francis. His story is not a whimsy, but a revelation of the archetypal Franciscan vocation. I don't think Francis had same-sex feelings of attraction, because there is no evidence to support such a claim that I know about. But he practised a rigorous honesty and never seemed to pull back from what he discovered about himself. We friars and sisters are giving birth to new generations, passing on the message of Franciscan spirituality to bring beauty, justice and peace to the world through social reproduction – our formation is revolutionary and can be passed on. The small, awkward beginnings – the tiny chapel of

Portiuncula and diminutive Assisi – truly underscore the fragility of the early Franciscan movement. Yet just about anything can happen if we are prayerful, passionate and live it honestly. Bill Wilson and Dr Bob, the founders of Alcoholics Anonymous, also started in shaky circumstances – nothing is shakier than a group of drunks until they grasp the new way of sober, prayerful living with life-or-death intensity.

'Francis and his brothers ...' It is a phrase that comes up repeatedly. Shortly after his conversion, as he was collecting stones and re-building San Damiano, men started to seek him out and join him: Peter, Bernard, Giles, Leo, Sylvester, Rufino, Masseo – within a few short years, thousands of men. Leo became particularly dear and important to him. Leo accompanied Francis on many of his travels and was in attendance nearby on Mount La Verna when Francis received the gift of the Lord's Stigmata – marks of the Crucifixion. In his *Testament* Francis wrote: 'And after the Lord gave me brothers, no one showed me what I should do, but the Most High Himself revealed to me that I should live according to the form of the Holy Gospel.' (Armstrong, Hellmann and Short, *Francis of Assisi*, vol. 1, p. 124). It was with his brothers, struggling with them, laughing with them, eating and working with them, that the founder's vision became realized. 'It is a life that is highly relational: one cannot be a Franciscan if he or she is not part of some sort of intimate and often quite complex network of relationships. "Loving one another is the heart of the Gospel Project as Francis and Clare understood it"' (McCormack, 'The Essential Elements of the Evangelical Life of Franciscans', p. 243). The Franciscan way of life became characterized by rigorous devotion and gentle compassion, fasts and feasts where the brothers were instructed to feed the birds and animals too. Singing and laughter are as much a distinguishing characteristic of Franciscan spirituality as silence.

I have lived among brothers for over 25 years. Many of the friars have been truly brothers to me, some senior to me, some my own age and younger. All have touched me deeply. Several different brothers are contemporaries of my father and have become like fathers to me, and we have had to thrash through my unresolved issues with my father when I have suddenly found myself reacting in weird and illogical ways to things they said to me. I have reacted to some with the special petulance of a rebellious teenager when I felt they were trying to control me. They are also great mentors. I'll never forget going on mission with one senior brother and watching him welcome people the first night. With a wide smile, arms open, he stood and sang 'This is holy ground ...'

A standout in my community life was my novice guardian, Jon. He was a moody one, but capable of great humour, love and understanding. We shared a passion for reading, and we loved to cook. He was a storyteller. He wasn't perfect: there was a painful episode when he failed in his celibate commitment and there was an official investigation. To our credit, we held him in our hearts and supported him in all that transpired. And to his credit, he stayed among us. Preaching at his funeral I didn't mention this failure because it felt inappropriate to the occasion. Perhaps I should have done, so that the true grit that is religious life could be held up in awe, penitence and gratitude as we remembered and gave thanks for his remarkable life.

Jon was a brilliant performance artist: puppetry and toy theatre was his medium. He was impatient with much of religious life while loving it. This awkward devotion was captured at the time of his death. I went to see him in the hospital, and he asked me, as Guardian, if he could die at home. Barely out of denial that he would die soon, I agreed, yet asked him *why*? We were none of us professional caregivers, wouldn't he be more comfortable somewhere else?

'That's the whole point,' he said. 'I joined a wacky group of guys and committed myself to our life together. I trust you to care for me to the best of your ability.' After a pause, he smiled, 'And I have no illusions about that.' His death came about four days later in the middle of the night. Tom and I were trying to get him up from the toilet, and he vomited, voided himself, and slumped in our arms. Surprised by the sudden weight, we slipped in the vomit, and all, and we fell to the floor in a heap, astounded. The Franciscan way of dying.

There are so many others I have loved deeply in the Order. Several have died. A few to whom I have felt particularly close have left the community; their departures were like unanaesthetized root canal operations. You can never second guess another person's vocational decisions. But I try not to let an inconvenient thing like feeling abandoned get in the way of brotherhood. There are some men who will always be my brothers no matter what, and their partners, wives and children an important part of my life. The Franciscan bond endures. Fortunately, we are a lively community around the world, and I am surrounded by love and encouragement.

As I ran back across the valley to Assisi, I tried to pick out the rooftop of the apartment where I was staying. I looked for different towers and cupolas as landmarks. The city on the hill is a remarkable sight; the whole expanse of it can be seen at a glance. Because of the life, ministry and ongoing intercession of Francis, this small city became and remains a place of blessing to many. According to Paul Sabatier, one of the great biographers partly responsible for the resurgence of interest in Francis in the nineteenth century:

Just before his death St Francis had himself carried on a litter to Saint Mary of the Portiuncula, so that there the life of his body would come to an end where he had begun to experience the light and life of his soul ... he asked those carrying the litter to place it on the ground. Since he could hardly see because of the serious and prolonged eye disease, he had the litter turned so that he would face the city of Assisi.

Raising himself up slightly on the litter, he blessed this city. 'Lord,' he said, 'just as, at an earlier time, this ancient city was, I believe, the place and abode of wicked and evil men, now I realize that, because of Your abundant mercy and in Your own time, You have singularly shown an abundance of Your mercies to it

... I ask you therefore, Lord Jesus Christ, Father of mercies, not to consider our ingratitude. Be mindful of Your most abundant piety which You have shown to it, that it always be an abode for those who truly acknowledge You, and glorify Your name blessed and most glorious forever and ever. Amen. (Armstrong, Hellmann and Short, *Francis of Assisi*, vol. 3, p. 372)

St Francis, it has been said, is the most admired and least emulated saint. My failure to live up to his example is beside the point, or rather should be assumed. My life task is to become fully myself, not a shadow of Francis. I value the examples of Francis and Clare very much but, as I have learned in sobriety, 'all-or-nothing' thinking is the real enemy of spiritual progress. I believe I am aided by their prayers and examples, and their goodness encourages me to do my best, relying on the grace of God. As the scripture says: '... he has made nothing incomplete. Each [one] supplements the virtues of the other ...' (Sirach 42.24b–42.25a) We're all connected.

As I gasped up the steeply stepped hillside to my home in Assisi, church bells rang, tourists called out to one another. I remembered Francis ended his life surrounded by song. As he lay on his bed the brothers sang his 'Canticle of the Creatures'. Creative to the last, he added a verse urging peace and reconciliation. Then he had himself moved naked to the floor, where he died in the evening. Then, the story goes, an exaltation of larks sang a resurrection song of the dawn and swirled around his cell, and the woods glowed with a great light.

As I approached the apartment, I hummed to myself: pleased, grateful, tired, rejuvenated, daunted and inspired by this man, my brother and father too. Rain streaked my face; other days the sun burned me, or wind made my eyes tear: 'Be praised, my Lord ... for all weathers.' And finally: 'Be praised, my Lord, for the storms of life with persecutions, the lash of addiction, the sweet grace of recovery: to you be praise, glory, honour and blessing.'

7

Testing the limits of forgiveness and reconciliation:
Haruro, Papua New Guinea

> The call to Christian living is a call to fix our eyes on the horizon
> of the new creation, a horizon marked by peace, justice, harmony
> and true life, and to 'live up' to that horizon, wrestling to live now
> as we will all live then. (Gooder, *Body*, p. 82)

On a July morning in 2015, I trot along the grassy *allée* through
Our Lady of the Angels Friary, Haruro, Oro Province, Papua New
Guinea, in the heart of the jungle. By the signpost at the head of
the lane is a crowing, red-wattled rooster. Chanticleer is aflame with
jewel-like feathers, gaudy macho gorgeousness like the Swiss Guards
I glimpsed once as I went to shake hands with Pope Francis after I'd
given a keynote speech at a Vatican symposium on the Consecrated
Life. 'It's nice to meet you, Sir,' I told the Pope.

The bird's iridescent black tail feathers arch and flutter like
a standard behind him. Standing sentry, he welcomes the
Sun King on a new day – 'De Colores!' as some would have
it. Around him, heads down, step his tawny-feathered wives,
docile attendants adorned with the gold of Ophir. Higher in
the rain tree and coconut palm canopy, I hear the irenic calls
of doves. As I run, I count the calls of white cockatoos, parrots,
and birds with names the brothers have taught me: gombus,
karakos, and the humble toilet-keeper – small black and white
birds who often feed near the latrines. High and low, birdsong

gives voice to a great hallelujah chorus. Papua New Guinea has documented 717 bird species. I am reminded of the famous painting by Giotto in Assisi of St Francis preaching to the birds. It is a reminder to the Franciscans of their mission to preach the gospel to all of creation, to the ends of the earth; these birds were doing their part in this steamy corner of Melanesia echoing the cry, 'Oro! Oro! Oro!' The local Oro Kaivo people sing: 'Welcome, welcome, welcome!' I have often been welcomed to the friary, not only with birdsong, but with men in loincloths and fantastic feather headdresses, beating drums, and bare-breasted women flapping tapa cloth shawls, showering me with flower petals, shouting 'Oro! Oro! Oro!'

I head up the dirt lane that goes up to the main, paved, road about half a mile away. On my right is Brother Sebastian's garden: 'Local, Papua New Guinea-style garden,' he laughingly explains as I stare bewildered at the tangle of burned-over tree trunks and scorched earth. Here and there, as space permits, he's planted taro suckers and aibika stems – *Abelmoschus manihot*, in the Latin. With the blackened wood and ground it looks post-apocalyptic. But green leaves poke up here and there, and I am reminded of the Easter song 'Now the green blade riseth … love is come again'.

I didn't always run alone. Once I was passing this way when I was joined on my run by three boys, two from the juvenile detention centre the brothers oversee for the National Department of Corrections, and a boy from a nearby palm-thatched house. If ever I am incarcerated, I hope I am kept by indulgent, friendly friars. These boys were lucky to end up at the friary where security functioned on the honour system and they had the run of the place like novices. Hearing their feet behind me, I turned and said, 'I'm running to Resurrection! Want to come?'

'Yes!' they chorused. 'We're the SSF cross-country team!' I told them. The Anglican Cathedral of the Resurrection was just over 3 miles away, a nice run.

I always feel honoured by the interest and trust of the younger brothers – some are only 22 years old – and other young people who seek me out from time to time. I like being a 'big brother'. We never know the impact we have on others. There is no dress rehearsal, as Malidoma Somé once said at a workshop about mentoring. 'There they are!' he explained. I must simply be the best I can in that moment. Being a guide and friend, I pay attention to these young men.

I can remember the men I looked up to outside my family as I was growing up. I was oblivious to much about them – their politics, for instance – but I was locked into their love and care for me. I had a few important men who taught me farming skills, beekeeping, 'the newspapering business'. They encouraged me to tackle small challenges and gave me praise that made me feel I counted for something, that I was a somebody. Sweetest of all was when they'd ask me questions and talk to me about what I thought. There were times when it felt they admitted me into the beautiful world of grown men, like when we were laughing, teasing or singing as we worked – not particularly beautifully, perhaps off-key, but manfully, light-heartedly. These were rare moments; they were busy people. But I can recall certain occasions with intense clarity and gratitude. In my memory, their judicious drawls still counsel me to be attentive, patient and careful when I face confounding circumstances. /

When I struggled with drink, the memory of these mentors made me hate myself; I knew I had failed them. But later when I was in recovery I spoke with those who were still alive and heard words of acceptance, respect and love. I'd been wrong about their imagined response to me. I don't know if they knew the impact they had on me.

We passed the cocoa bean 'fermentary', a corrugated-iron-clad building, blooming with rust. I helped push a barrow of beans up to the fermentary one year. Cocoa is a nice little moneymaking project for the friary. The brothers and local farmers bring their freshly harvested cocoa beans to be packed in wooden troughs, covered with banana leaves, and allowed to ferment. After three days, the beans have turned from white, in a sweet, milky substance, to a rich dark brown. They are shovelled on to large wire trays to dry, and to be exposed to heat – sun from above and fire beneath. The facility has the sweet yeasty, rotting smell of a brewery, with base notes of damp fireplace.

We were running to the Cathedral of the Resurrection, but it seemed to me everything around us had a message of resurrection – rooster, vegetables leafing out, healing companionship. A kaleidoscope of lemon-yellow butterflies scattered from the damp, muddy road as we approached. An imperial-sized electric-blue butterfly cut across our path. From egg to caterpillar, then hidden in its tomb-like chrysalis, emerging finally as a radiant adult butterfly, the life cycle of the butterfly is one of complete metamorphosis. It is possible that every church school bulletin board in the world has cut-out butterflies, symbols of the Resurrection. Recovery literature and art also use the butterfly with its promise of transformation and new life.

The lane cuts through the jungle alive with a soundtrack of calling birds and buzzing wasps, bordered by tall grass stirred by the cyclone-fomenting butterfly wings. It is a road to renewal. But I have discovered even beautiful or inspiring long-distance vistas can enervate and distract me. The best way to close the gap between me and any end point is to keep my attention focused on the ground beneath my feet, looking out for stones and puddles, appreciating the plants I am passing. Especially going uphill, I need to look down – it helps me stay focused.

The boys and I reached the end of the lane and hit the blacktop road and began to settle into a slow steady pace – one, two, three, four – that helps me cover long distances. I forget the pace nearly every day and set off too fast. Recovering myself is an exercise in mindfulness and remembering. When I slip into my natural pace, I can relax – shoulders back, my legs supporting the run.

We pressed on. We crossed a bridge over a creek, then another over a smaller stream. We ran silently. I loved hearing the boys breathe, their feet pounding along the road with me. We kept together, each of us beginning to sweat heavily in the intense heat. I caught one boy's eye – he smiled and gave me a thumbs-up.

Rank upon rank of oil palm trees line the road, interspersed with plots of dead ones, poisoned to make room for a new generation of trees. In some parts of Asia, the monoculture of oil palm threatens the environment. It degrades the vitality of biodiversity, and there is evidence that the witch's brew of poisons has leached into the water supply. From the air, it is obvious that significant plots of land have been given over to oil palm production in Oro Province, as well as other parts of Papua New Guinea.

Whatever the liabilities, the locals consider the plantations good places to work. With knives and saw blades attached to long poles they groom the trees, cutting away dead branches. The dimpled trunks host lush ferns and philodendron-like plants, creating a lacy-leafed pavilion with vaulting green pillars. When the fruit appears bright red on top, they cut down the clusters and collect them on large nets that are gathered up by trucks and taken for processing. The brothers tell me it is very hard work – no surprise there. A nightmarish part for me would be the snakes that come tumbling down with the fruit clusters. 'Some of the workers eat them, too!' a brother told me with a shudder. One man's poison is another man's meat.

We ran on, our bodies burning our banana calories; the staple food ration is almost 24 bananas every day per man – of several different kinds and sizes. We eat other things too, but bananas are king. Finally, we reached a crossroads. A sign stated that Kokoda was 48 miles to the left, and Popondetta a mile straight ahead. We stopped to breathe and sip water.

This crossroads, I have been told, is near to the place where some Japanese soldiers bayoneted two Australian women during World War Two. One was a teacher, Mavis Parkinson, and the other was a nurse, May Hayman, called 'sister' after the fashion of calling nurses 'sister'. They were Gona missionaries from the Anglican Church of Australia. Bishop Philip Strong, the Anglican Archbishop of New Guinea, gave a rousing radio speech that was broadcast to the missionaries working in Papua New Guinea during the war.

He said: 'No, my brothers and sisters, fellow workers in Christ, whatever others may do, we cannot leave. We shall not leave. We shall stay by our trust. We shall stand by our vocation. We do not know what it means to us. Many already think us fools and mad. What does it matter? If we are fools, "we are fools for Christ's sake"' (Carr Rowland, *Faithful Unto Death*). I wonder what I would say? Xavier Beauvois's 2010 prize-winning film *Of Gods and Men* raises the same question as a group of monks in Algeria chose not to flee the fighting there. It was an agonizing decision. They were kidnapped by terrorists and then assassinated during the Algerian civil war in 1996. Could I carry the cross to such an end?

The missionaries in New Guinea, like the monks in Algeria, stayed out of loyalty to the people they served who had no option of fleeing the invading Japanese. They were betrayed by some local people who hoped to find favour with the Japanese. A small boy – now a very old man – followed the Japanese soldiers who dragged off the two women. I am told by the brothers that he climbed a breadfruit tree and watched the soldiers rape the women, then bayonet them, one in the throat and the other in the stomach. The women were buried in a very shallow, careless grave near the crossroads. A year later the boy led some Americans to the place. They exhumed the bodies – which showed remarkably little decomposition – and moved them and reburied them beneath an altar-like monument further down the road. We passed the shrine as we approached the cathedral.

Brooding over this story, I could feel the hungry rat of anger and hate begin to gnaw at my stomach, taking sides in a conflict long finished. I breathed a prayer to the Holy Spirit to check my self-righteousness. Stoking hate and partisanship were not the lessons I wanted to give the boys, nor to take for myself from these memories. The memory of another young woman caught up in World War Two helped me.

Etty Hillesum was a young Jewish woman held at the Westerbork transit camp, who finally died at Auschwitz. She determined not to allow her heart and her life to be destroyed by hate, writing in her diary: 'Why should we always have to choose the cheapest and easiest way? It has been brought home forcibly to me here how every atom of hatred added to the world makes it an even more inhospitable place' (Woodhouse, *Etty Hillesum*, p. 75). She decided to keep God and God's love and the awareness of the fragile beauty of the earth alive in that forecourt of hell.

Her diaries preserve the record of her life in the camp, her suffering, and how she lived out her commitment to keep living gratefully until her life was over. As the train carrying her and her family left the camp bound for Auschwitz, she pushed a card addressed to a friend through the boards of the cattle wagon. A farmer picked it up and sent it on. On it, she wrote ' ... In the end the departure came without warning. On sudden orders from The Hague. We left the camp singing ...' (Woodhouse, *Etty Hillesum*, p. 131)

Dividing the world into good people and bad people is a dead end, though obviously there are very bad actions and attitudes with which we cannot make peace. Hating people doesn't serve the gospel. At the same time, we must always work against violence, hateful rhetoric and propaganda, actions and attitudes that hurt and diminish others. Taking the opportunity to practise looking at the world with a larger, more generous vision is an act of redemption which, as Paula Gooder points out, is the purpose of resurrection. This devotional rest stop on our run was worth it, because it reminded me that some actions are hateful in the extreme, but I don't want to be captive to hate. I must work for greater understanding among people.

Recognizing there were other missionaries from different denominations who lost their lives, the mingled blood of the New Guinea martyrs is one of the arguments for church unity (see *Unitatis Redintegratio, 1965*, Second Vatican Council Decree on Ecumenism). They all endured a time of great danger when they prayerfully chose to serve the people among whom they lived rather than leave for safety. They died in fidelity to their Christian ministry. Nobody can say the witness of one denomination was truer than that of another in a situation like that. Denominationalism is beside the point and their deaths are a prompt to the Church to keep on living into that larger reality. At the resurrection from the dead, it won't matter which denomination we belonged to, only our love and faithfulness to Christ. The chapel at Martyrs' School is dedicated to them all.//

In 1991 the Archbishop of Canterbury, George Carey, came to Papua New Guinea and visited the grave and the school. He also received a delegation of descendants of the local families who had collaborated with the Japanese. Their collaboration had contributed to the martyrdoms of 11 Anglicans, as well as missionaries of other denominations and native converts to Christianity, but to say they were responsible would be overstating the case by far. The heartfelt and tearful apology of the families to the Archbishop of Canterbury, and to representatives of the families of the missionaries, was a significant moment in the long, long process of healing from the ravages and confusion of the war.

Asking for forgiveness and making amends was one of the hardest things I did in early sobriety; it loomed larger in my imagination than telling all to my sponsor. Confessing to a priest or confidant was familiar enough but sitting with people I felt I had harmed scared me. One person said: 'You always say, Sorry, Sorry! Just stop behaving that way!' His bracing comment was the only one like it of the many responses I received, and still he showed me extraordinary kindness and generosity. I found I could finally look people in the eye with confidence and affection.

My sponsor, who had heard many of my stories of community life, added one name when I was telling him the list of people I had harmed. 'Don't add him!' I objected strenuously. 'He owes me an apology. Why should I make amends for what he did to me?' In the confident way of one who has been down this road, my friend observed that this might be the most important person on my list.

I would discover in due time what I was to say. At that point, I had been harbouring a resentment that crouched like an evil homunculus in me, spewing forth the tale of my victimization at every mention of his name for about eight years. Several years later – what was I doing? – suddenly I found myself thinking of him and realized he had been reacting to my alcohol-fuelled behaviour. As I have learned in recovery, my bad behaviour often brought out the worst in others.

Suddenly the camouflage of resentment and denial was pulled back to reveal my culpability. I felt ashamed of all the things I'd said before, and I knew what I wanted to say to him. But we were separated by a continent and I figured we would never cross paths again. 'Just wait,' my sponsor said.

Another few years passed. I was participating in a workshop when I looked up to see him in the audience. With a dry throat and sweaty palms, I approached him at the break. 'Hello,' I said, hardly able to meet his eyes because I was trying to hide my emotion. After a panicked pause, I launched into my explanation of the new directions in my life, and the recognition of how my behaviour had put him in a difficult position.

Stumbling to a stop, I took a deep breath and offered him my hand, finally looking him straight in the eyes. Not knowing what he would do or say, I pumped his hand vigorously. 'I am so happy for what is happening in your life,' he said. 'Of course, I forgive you, I just hope you can forgive me!' Practically hysterical with relief, I began blinking back tears furiously. We hugged. Over a decade of alcoholic rage and resentment drained away.

My sweaty gang pushed on towards Resurrection Cathedral. The large open-sided steel structure with a corrugated iron roof is extremely simple, but the utilitarian building is imbued with holiness: cross, altar, pulpit, are all there. Signs of weekly worship: a hymn board, wilted flowers in a vase, children's artwork taped to the wall, flapping in the breeze. It was blissful to sit in the cool shade, and rest. Although I usually focus on the exigencies, the troubles, it is important to remember that my life is full of moments of respite.

Finally, we stood and stretched our legs, preparing to run back. We dithered, admiring the well-tended football pitch behind the Cathedral School. It too is a holy place where hopes and dreams converge. The Church is like a playing field where we practise our Christian life – where, as Eugene Peterson says, we practise resurrection living.

All of us felt reluctant to leave our shady sanctuary next to the Cathedral. I tried to re-frame it for us: 'We aren't running a race. Nobody is forcing us to do this. We are doing this for fun!' I couldn't believe how much I could hear the voice of my parents as I spoke, cajoling us to enjoy holiday outings in the rain. 'We're having fun!' I finished lamely. 'Let's just do our best, take it slowly, and rest as we need to.' Survivor's counsel.

We started back out of the Cathedral garth to the town road. The heat was worse than before, and I began to accuse myself: 'Mad dogs and *Americans* go out in the noonday sun ...' We darted from one cool pool of shade to the next; soon it seemed we were playing a game and the teenagers began to laugh. I laughed too – eventually.

Returning to the friary we flopped on the grass, clothing sopping wet with sweat. The two boys from the detention centre seemed happy. 'My other prison in Port Moresby was much bigger than this place,' one of them said. 'The warden was always organizing sports,' he said wistfully. 'We ran, played games. Here we don't do sport very much. With you, this was our first run.'

Later, one of the boys came to me as I was drying dinner dishes. 'I want something from you, to remember you. I'll probably never see you again.' I gave him my cross.

I can't imagine life any better than this. It is a second chance for me, and for those boys. The beauty of the forests and plantations, the sounds of birds, people laughing, the chance to remember and practise the essential skills of my faith: forgiveness, compassion, time to play in the sun. This is the abundant life Jesus promised us.

8

Claiming the power of God's blessings: Dorset, England

> A view of the world that splits the body from the soul, and vice versa, can maintain a fundamental difference between what you do and what you think. Paul is clear that there is no divide; what you do affects what you think; what you think affects what you do. (Gooder, *Body*, p. 100)

A bell and a tree stand at the entrance of the Friary of St Francis at Hilfield, Dorset, England. The bell is very old, and the tree is very young. They are compelling symbols of two aspects of the Franciscan vocation of the Society of St Francis. The bell is unassumingly ancient, hanging humbly in a ground-level frame. She might be medieval. I am thrilled by her antiquity – this bell is a treasure, one of the finer things in the Order's possession. This Dowager Duchess of a gong rules the roost too; she's the chapel bell. To ring her, the sacristan must go 25 yards or so to her in all weathers like a supplicant begging a favour. Pulling her heavy rope elicits a rich, reverberating sound. It is an authoritative sound, with a perfect pitch, like a proper bell is supposed to sound. Hearing the bell reminds me of the time I received a card commanding me to attend a Garden Party at Buckingham Palace. This old bell elegantly commands attendance at prayer.

The tree, planted near the bell, is only 62 years old. It is no sapling, but still 250 years younger than the evocatively named Gospel Oak growing in Longmeadow behind the friary. The

English love oak trees. Millions were used to build the vessels of the Royal Navy; more have been incorporated into homes, from cottages to castles. Shakespeare imagined soldiers camouflaged as oaks in the stealth attack on Macbeth. Now, on behalf of a grateful nation, the most ancient specimens are named and protected as part of the national heritage.

This friary oak is an oak of righteousness, despite its youth. It was a gift to one of our founding brothers, Brother Douglas, from German prisoners-of-war among whom he ministered in Germany after World War Two. Their prayer was for friendship to grow between Great Britain and Germany with the life of the tree. At the time, it was a risky and honourable sentiment, and reminds me of our Franciscan vocation to leap across prejudice and social barriers, to call the rulers of the world to reconciliation.

It is also a monument to the integrity of Brother Douglas, who ministered with real compassion among those soldiers of a fallen enemy, winning their trust and friendship. The story belongs in the same canon as the meeting of St Francis with the robbers of Sansepolcro, or the story of the Wolf of Gubbio, when, through generosity in both cases, Francis brokered simple peace agreements. With God's help, enemies are only potential friends.

With only a few hours before the bell sounds for evensong, I run double-time out of the friary past the bell and tree with my imagination leaping six months ahead. I'd just volunteered to work during January among refugees – Syrians, Iranians, Eritreans, Sudanese and whatever other unfortunate souls – in Calais, France. I wonder what friends I might make. I turn left on to one of my favourite English routes, and run down a Franciscan highway, of sorts. It is, fittingly, a no-name road, but one that has ushered countless men and women into the world to preach peace, to lend a hand, to sing God's praises.

Some, with frayed hems and ropes flapping at their sides, went out as brothers. Others have been people who, after time at the friary, have been sent on their way restored, healed and forgiven. Over the decades, the road has also delivered to the friary foot-sore wayfarers and overwhelmed clerics from up and down the Anglican hierarchy seeking respite. Sometimes it has been a flood of visitors: men and women simply wanting a chance to breathe and pray and enjoy the beautiful chapel, meadows, woods and the community's what-you-see-is-what-you-get hospitality offered to all comers.

In its early history, the place was built – in 1888 – as a shooting lodge for the Earl of Sandwich. Gradually it was transformed from a bastion of establishment privilege to a house of innovation – and eventually gospel values – that challenged anybody who liked the way things have always been done. The hunting lodge became a frontier for social change. In the early twentieth century George Montague, the nephew and heir of the eighth Earl of Sandwich, founded 'The Little Commonwealth', an experimental residential school for children.

An impressive legacy of this time is a couple of houses that the children helped to build, and an avenue of lime trees – *Tilia x europaea* in Latin – that lead down to the present-day cemetery. Once when I was visiting, a group of Asian tourists showed up, educators who had heard about the Little Commonwealth and wanted to see it. Then in 1919 the children's school became a training centre for ex-soldiers. Finally, in 1921, a fledgling Anglican Franciscan order moved in, eventually to become the Society of St Francis. (For a thorough and highly engaging description of the founding of the Society of St Francis, see Petà Dunstan, *This Poor Sort*)

Today Hilfield Friary has a registered herd of Shetland cattle. There are also Dorset sheep, and chickens that are moved around in a rustic *wagon-lit*. Pigs come and go frequently – into the sty to fatten up and out on to the table for supper. Most of the friars aren't vegetarians; but they are committed to local, organic and sustainable food. The premises comprise at least eight buildings on close to 50 acres of land.

The resident community includes six or seven friars, several young volunteers from various places around the globe, longer-term community members who may be married or single and not necessarily vowed religious, and also people needing a safe place to live for a while. In all, about 24 people call the friary home. At the centre of their common life, they pray in the old farm stables, a long, narrow, sloping-floored chapel that seems just right for the community members gathered with mud-caked jeans and damp woollen jerseys. Outside the windows in summer, roses wave in the casements.

I trot past Flowers Farm on my left with its sign about trout ponds. As I make my way downhill, I glimpse fields on both sides, of the ilk of more celebrated English vistas captured by John Constable and other landscape artists. I love losing myself in Constable's huge paintings when I see them in museums, and running through this Dorset countryside it feels as if I have leaped through a gilded frame into an enchanted land. You either love the countryside or you don't. I am a fan.

Cattle and sheep chew the cud, rabbits nibble warily, birds sing in the bushes – I hear what I decide are mating calls; what else are they shouting about? I see hares and badger setts, but I've never seen a badger as I don't run at night. The ditch gurgles, and in places the water leaps out of the shallow channel and floods the road. The lichen-crusted Hilfield church dedicated to St Nicholas stands visible on the brow of a hill, worn by wind and rain at the corners like a salt lick.

This area of Dorset is 'Hardy country', written about by Thomas Hardy in his novels. In *Tess of the d'Urbervilles*, writing what seems like a description of the route I run, Hardy says:

Here in the valley, the world seems to be constructed upon a smaller and more delicate scale, the fields are mere paddocks, so reduced that from this height their hedgerows appear a network of dark green threads overspreading the paler green of the grass. The atmosphere below is languorous, and it is so tinged with azure that what artists call the middle distance partakes of that hue whilst the horizon beyond is of deepest ultramarine. (p. 5)

The countryside does indeed look beautiful and languorous, and I can feel almost drunk on the 'fatness and warm ferments' that Hardy mentions elsewhere. I love to count the familiar plants, so similar to my native Washington State on the West Coast in the States: elderberry, blackberry, nettles, burdock, hazel, wild rose, dandelion and thistles are the ones I can confidently identify.

There are many other plants in the madcap flourishing of the Dorset hedgerows. It's beautiful, but you can't let your guard down. The scene can change rapidly. In Hardy's novel, the unfortunate Tess goes from singing happily one day in the early morning sunshine to – just months later – chopping turnips in the gelid mud. As I crest a hill and slither into cow manure smeared all over the road, my reverie is broken. Shocked into attentiveness by the smell of the 'warm ferments', I frantically tip-toe around the slippery greenish pats.

Once, on a run along these roads, I got caught up in a herd of cattle being moved from one paddock to another. Dogs barked at their heels, boys whistled and shouted. Manure splattered my shins. I was reminded of very similar circumstances when I was a young teenager, working at my first job. We were herding cattle along the road, the herd being led by Dundee, the enormous Hereford bull. As the animals trotted towards me, where I stood at an intersection with a private driveway, I was gripped by panic and wet myself. The experience was deeply shaming for a 13-year-old boy. Perhaps because the animals stayed on the road, and because of being put in those circumstances again and again, I gradually mastered my fear around cattle. I spent every Saturday morning for years scraping down a small cattle feedlot.

Then I took a job on a farm with horses and mucked out the stables – somebody else handled the animals. Initially the faecal smells were revolting. Eventually I didn't notice the smells, astonishingly enough. Perhaps it was only that the brain began to register it differently: 'this is what money smells like' to a cash-strapped teenager. Just as running used to be unimaginable misery, now it is a joy.

It is amazing what one can get used to when we re-frame our context, use different criteria to denote what is important. It has been an incredibly slow process for me. But gradually, I have taken my fears on, one by one, naming and facing a legion of gremlins, things I have construed as making me less acceptable, less worthy than other boys and men. Unathletic, afraid of cows and horses, ashamed of wetting myself, afraid of coming out with my sexual preference, worried what others think of me.

It is like an archaeological dig where the most important work is done with brushes and feathers, not spades. I can't triumph over these demons by fiat – yet I can see the hallmarks of Jesus' involvement, blessing me, gathering me up, showing me the way forward through the help of many people who taught me how to live faithfully, how to see life differently, and gave me courage.

Even though I don't have a magical or miraculous cure for low self-esteem, fear, or anything else that has ailed me, I believe I have been healed in ways that have restored me to a deeper sense of wholeness. While I still feel fearful from time to time, I don't freeze up and pee in my pants. I've learned I can breathe into the fears and open them up a bit, giving myself time to recollect. Often enough there is a hiccough in time before I move through a fearful reaction, until I remember I have no reason to fear cows or other people.

Once I'd had the flashback to that day 44 years ago, I remember it every time I run this route and I pray for that scared boy. The memory has become a spiritual touchstone for me. I welcome any moves towards freedom from a me-centred or just panic-driven life. Among people I only need to open my mouth and speak, creating a relationship by merely confessing my awkwardness, which time and again is received with laughter and understanding. Fear healed. Among cattle I bluster and slap flanks. It is now like heaven to mix with them. As one of my friends says: 'The unconditional yes is hospitality to life in any guise in which it visits us … it can be an indication of the holiness of things. Holiness is wholeness' (Richo, *The Five Things We Cannot Change*, p. 4).

When I am on the Dorset roads, my thoughts are not far from the wayfarers that the brothers served. They were homeless men who walked the roads during the first half of the twentieth century. Most had served during World War One and couldn't readjust to life during peacetime, suffering what I suppose we would now call post-traumatic stress disorder. Doubtless there were many reasons for them to seek out casual labour and the freedom of the roads. Society provided almost nothing in the way of support and few options for mental rehabilitation, so perhaps they felt doomed to it. At every crossroads near the Dorset friary, there are signs pointing to 'The Friary'. It is an open invitation to come and rest. For years and years wayfarers were welcomed, given food and a place to stay, included in the life and prayers of the brothers. This ministry waned as the government stepped up to its obligations to help the poor and homeless. But whenever I pass a sign, I feel proud of the friary's local visibility.

Those extraordinary pioneering friars farmed, cared for wayfarers, welcomed many diverse visitors, all the while keeping a regular rhythm of prayer. The first leader was Brother Giles, and he was succeeded by Brother Douglas. As it was later in his work among German prisoners-of-war, Brother Douglas from the start showed an easy, welcoming manner to the wayfarers. I've heard many stories about how he welcomed them all as 'brothers' and encouraged them to eat with the community.

During the day, they worked hard farming. Even more telling of the lengths to which he resorted to serve the wayfarers is the fact that Brother Douglas sometimes tramped the roads himself, sharing the lot of the men. Nothing authenticates a social critique and vision like a shared, lived experience. Moving from his comfort zone to the Kingdom zone preached by Jesus, the experience of wayfaring moved Douglas from indignation at the way society treated the poor, and veterans as well, to compassionate loving-kindness and political engagement.

I remember standing outside the Houses of Parliament in Westminster in 2011, listening to the eminent scholar Petà Dunstan tell the challenging story of Douglas's advocacy of reform of the Poor Laws and the treatment of vagrants. In 1929 Douglas gave evidence to the Parliamentary Commission on Vagrancy, representing the Vagrancy Reform Society. Although sleeping out in hedgerows and 'in the rough' remained illegal until 1935, Douglas and others won improvements in the conditions in the casual labour wards, calling for better diet, regular medical check-ups, an end to stone-breaking, and the provision of separate sleeping cubicles in the wards (Dunstan, *This Poor Sort*, p. 58). He, along with many others, set the bar very high for Franciscan ministry in our community.

Finally, I come to a road with a name: Load Lane. Fields of hay run out on both sides of the road, escaping from beneath enormous trees. I lay down my mental burdens on Load Lane and pick up the pace because the road slopes down slightly. A song buzzes in my brain: 'I'm gonna lay down my sword and shield …' I always thank God for the grace of surrender when I put down the drink and bad feelings. Even more, I thank God for companions on the road to freedom – my Franciscan brothers and sisters, and another community of recovering drunks who are unfailingly frank and compassionate, challenging the games I play on myself, and sometimes others.

At the Batcombe Road crossroads, I turn left again to Wriggle River Lane. One of the brothers pointed out to me that, odd as it sounds, the stream's Italian name would be Rivo Torto. That's a familiar Franciscan place name. It is where Francis took shelter with his first companions in a barn, faithful to his desire to emulate the Son of Man who had nowhere to lay his head.

The unsympathetic farmer, perhaps alarmed by these rich kids running around in rags and disrupting the received order of things, backed his donkey in among the sleeping friars and drove them out into the fields. Poor brothers!

Nevertheless, it is encouraging to think about what a body can endure when the mind and heart are on fire with an ideal. I'm fairly confident I could cope with tramping the roads, but it would require extra prayers to remain happy and undisturbed by ticks, bedbugs, scabies, the threat of being robbed, the lurking threat of illness. Modern analogies might be the experience of boot camp, which would be unendurable, I suppose, without patriotism and fellow aspiring soldiers to leaven the hardships. Religious life would be a ridiculous misery without the experience of God's love and the continuous affirmation of brothers and sisters firing us up for the challenges we face.

Also, like the cranky farmer, many people then and now are legitimately wary of seeming fanatics with their heads full of ideas and their hearts confused – or, worse, full of hate. It took Francis a while to be recognized and welcomed by the population in general and the Church of his day. What authenticated those early brothers was their uncomplaining perseverance and sincere gratitude for whatever they were given, discerning God's mercy even if all they got was sticks and stones: they were even grateful for the chastisement of their bodies. As I mulled over these thoughts of the vulnerability of the Franciscan life and our concomitant strengths, I once again listed for myself my powers: the power to love, to laugh, to help, to forgive, to breathe in times of stress, to pray always, to hold the fearful, to speak encouragingly, to weep with the sad and lonely, to share food, to tell stories, to choose what I disclose, to offer companionship, to remain stolid and unmoved by bluster and threats, to make friends, to run, to cheer, to sit quietly, to learn new skills, to think, to learn new attitudes, to trust God's providence, to endure provocation and persecution – should it ever come. St Francis embodied these powers, and we don't always have to dig too deeply to discover them – and more – in ourselves. We are powerful.

The River Wriggle is about halfway on the route, and from there back to the friary property it is all a gentle upward incline. The road is basically straight as it heads towards Batcombe. The steady rhythm of my running quietens my mind. I love the endorphin-fuelled feeling of wellbeing. My heart beats strongly. Even in the cool afternoon mist I feel warm. On the front of my thighs my quadricep muscles feel supple. Sometimes when I run, I hunch forward, and my trapezoid muscle framing my neck and shoulders tightens, leading to stabbing pain in my shoulders and neck. As I ease into my pace, I do my body inventory, reminding myself to relax my shoulders, straighten my back, keep my head up. Running is not just about legs; the whole body contributes to the effort. I find that it is only with head, neck and back comfortably aligned that I can run smoothly.

As I approach the intersection with Great Head Lane my steps slow. Turning left again, the road inclines steeply uphill for several hundred yards. It is one of the longest steeply graded roads I run anywhere in the world. Only my route in South Korea, and another route in the Solomon Islands over Snake Hill, are more toilsome. The hill claims my whole attention. I am called back to the immediate moment. I know I can run the distance, though it requires extra concentration and a rhythmic chant: 'Trust and obey … Trust and obey ….' At the top, I have to stop and pant, and having caught my breath I can admire the view of the South Downs. It is one of the greatest blessings of running outdoors in some of the most beautiful countryside I know.

Some of the wooded areas around the friary are recorded in the Domesday Book. They may look bucolic and peaceful, but these lush, green, sheep-spangled fields and copses have histories that are harsh. The brothers have reminded me that the view has changed dramatically over the years. Long ago the land was populated by many more people. With the enclosure movement, people were driven off. Industrialization then lured them to the cities and to an entirely different kind of life – and, as Charles Dickens, F. D. Maurice and others have pointed out, in many cases to misery.

At the top of the rise along Great Head Lane, the trees crouch over the road like runners leaning into the last lap. Here the Hilfield Community has been restoring the woods by coppicing the trees. This means they cut them down near the ground in order to encourage them to put out new shoots. It's an ancient sustainable way of managing the forest. They have also begun remaking the hedgerows. I saw with pleasure the simple weave they have used, lacing the slim trunks together in a tight pattern that discourages the most intrepid ewe or cow. The smell of wild garlic is strong in the damp glades. It makes me hungry and I sprint along the old drover road cut into the hill that borders the friary land to the entrance.

Running down the friary lane past the upper field is always rejuvenating. It is a relief to be going downhill. Because the field hasn't been ploughed in a very long time, it is home to eight species of English orchids. When I first learned this, I went looking for the flashy blooms I knew so well in the tropics. But these orchids are as understated as English country folk. You must look hard to find them, and bend down cosily to see their beauty. They reward affectionate scrutiny. Nestled among the grasses you can spot small clusters of purple flowers, sometimes tiny yellow stars, blooms that look like bees: fragile, beautiful, full of the glory of God.

Jesus hung an important teaching on the beauty of the flowers of the field: '(Consider how) they neither toil nor spin, yet I tell you, even Solomon in all his glory was not clothed like one of these.' (Matthew 6.28–29) Worry, overwork, the default behaviours of many human beings, only take us away from God. It is not that we should sit around doing nothing, but we must aim towards the goal of acting without fretting or pique or even a sense of self-reliance, hubris or as a bargain with God. The fact that everything changes with time – both the seasons and the passing of the years – makes the present moment even more important.

To live in and enjoy the present moment is a spiritual destiny worth the surrender of all our worries. St James contemplates flowers, too, finding a warning to the rich: 'The rich will disappear like a flower in the field. For the sun rises with its scorching heat and withers the field; its flower falls, and its beauty perishes. It is the same with the rich; in the midst of a busy life, they will wither away' (James 1.10–11). Better to seek spiritual satisfactions for happiness.

The well-heeled have always had a place in Christian life – sharing their wealth for the spread of the gospel. It's not having money that is the problem, but how one thinks about it and uses it. Spend it on helping people! There are no conditions attached to the love and care of God. Just as the rain and the sun fall on the just and the unjust, so God cares for the poor and rich alike. There is no contest for God's love. We don't compete for it. We don't earn it by taking a vow of poverty. Nor is being rich a sign of special favour. If anything, it's the reverse. In so many situations in the Bible it is the poor who are favoured. God particularly hears their cry. And at Christmas we remember Jesus was born not in a palace, but in a stable, and rested in a manger.

Humans exist as part of creation; we exist because God takes delight in us. Running has heightened the pleasure I take in life and helped to clear my head. With a clearer head, I have discovered a way to live more simply. And, I believe, more effectively: 'What you do affects what you think; what you think affects what you do,' as Gooder teaches (*Body*, p. 100). Take time, then, to delight in the flowers, to smell the garlic, and to breathe deeply the rich smells of the countryside. There is time for all these things. Even in the busiest life, there is time for everything our bodies and our souls need. There is a time to look and a time to work; a time to pray and a time to celebrate; a time for sport and a time for music; a time to eat and a time to rest; a time to serve and a time to be served. There is a time for going out into the world and a time for coming home.

9

Living a sane and sober life in the midst of turmoil: Jerusalem, Israel

Resisting the dualisms that are thrown across our path is never easy but it is very important to do … Proclaim redemption whenever and wherever we see it. (Gooder, *Body*, p. 47)

Although my preferred approach to a new city is to wander aimlessly, calling myself a *flâneur* when I want to elevate my practice, on this once-in-a-lifetime chance to visit Jerusalem, I had specific experiences in mind. High on my agenda was to run around the walls of the Old City. I wanted to fulfil a daydream I'd had since I started reading the Psalter, 40 years ago: to make the circuit of Zion, walk round about her; count the number of her towers. At my ordination to the priesthood the choir sang for the Introit C. H. H. Parry's 'I was glad when they said unto me … Our feet shall stand in thy gates, O Jerusalem' (1902). This anthem became the mental soundtrack to my visit. Head ringing with music about Jerusalem and how unity overcomes division, I prowled the sites important to me, looking for meaningful moments. Gladly I watched the people and spent time particularly in the Holy Sepulchre and the market in the Old City.

My home base in Jerusalem was the Monastery of St Saviour, an ancient Franciscan friary at 1 St Francis Street in the old city. The Franciscan presence in the Middle East began when St Francis famously travelled to Egypt in 1219. This holy fool decided the only way to end the Crusade was to convert the Sultan. If he failed, he harboured a hope for martyrdom – commendable in a way in terms of his complete surrender to God, but it makes me nervous to point this out in the twenty-first century. Fortunately, his guileless nature charmed the Sultan and their friendship circumvented any self-sacrificing jihadi leaning Francis had. They discovered respect for each other and a way to relate amicably with storytelling and prayer ('Chronicle of Ernoul', in Armstrong, Hellmann and Short, *Francis of Assisi* vol. 1, pp. 605–7). If only this could become the template for resolving religious conflict and power struggles in the world today. After this encounter, Francis encouraged his brothers to live among the Muslims without seeking their conversion.

From this ancient connection grew a ministry that endures to this day. Father Artemio Vitores, vicar of the Franciscan Custody at the time of my visit and also my host, once gave an interview explaining the Franciscan presence in the Holy Land:

The Franciscans desired to be at the service of all, Christians and Muslims, and showed that they had a modern universalistic spirit ahead of their time.

The protection of the holy sites was the fundamental reason for the Franciscan presence in the Holy Land, which they exercised through enormous difficulties and conflicts. The Franciscans initiated a social service of assistance and formation around the sites.

In the reception hall of our convent, there are five paintings that exemplify the Franciscans' mission in the Holy Land. Among these, there are two portraits of Robert of Anjou and Sancha of Majorca, sovereigns of Naples, who acquired the Cenacle from the Sultan of Egypt in 1333, and gave it to the Franciscans, who established their first monastery there.

In 1342, Pope Clement IV institutionalized the mission of the Franciscan Custody in the Holy Land.[1]

My first day in the city was a Sunday and I was off to church. I clattered down the shadowy back staircase of St Saviour's and ran out into the eye-searing December morning. Predictably, I sneezed several times. 'It's your residual caveman reaction to sunlight,' a friend once commented. I pinched my nostrils to clear them with a snort as I was taught by farmhands when I was 13. I jogged up the steep driveway to the gate house where the guard waved and smiled, then through to New Gate in the Old City wall.

I heard bells ringing. A muezzin's voice soared. In resonant haunting beauty even with the distortions of the loudspeakers he pleaded, calling the faithful to prayer. In the dark alleyways 'Jingle Bells' blared from shop fronts. In the Holy City you can run, but you can't hide from Santa Claus and the admonition to get ready for Christmas – meaning buy, buy, buy! Right in front of the monastery, the Christian Arab Boy Scout bagpipe and drum corps practised a marching piece – over and over *fortissimo*. Pigeon wings stuttered. People muttered, cajoled and laughed. The reveille sounds of the Old City of Jerusalem urged me on. I was off to find St George's Anglican Cathedral in East Jerusalem.

At the door of the Anglican Cathedral I was astonished to be greeted by a woman who demanded: 'Which one are you?'

After a moment of confusion, I recognized the cross around her neck that proclaimed her membership of the Society of St Francis Third Order. 'Clark.'

'Oh! I've been praying for you for seven years!' she said. What a great way to begin a friendship. Later she confided that she'd assumed any habited friar in the Anglican Cathedral in Jerusalem would likely be a member of SSF.

We arranged to meet after the liturgy. It turned out Ann was in Jerusalem to prepare for a pilgrimage she was to help facilitate in a year's time. Although an experienced traveller and frequent visitor to Jerusalem, she wanted to experience the climate at that time of year, size of the crowds, and any other contingencies first hand. So, she took me under her care and showed me around the city, inviting me to go to places I might otherwise have passed up: for instance, the cisterns under the city and a tunnel under the Western wall.

On my own, I ran among people in the shadows at the base of the craggy walls of the Old City. I was enfiladed by images in rapid fire. At one corner, I felt as though I could be in Manhattan with coffee shops and young people in jeans and hoodies; then, I stumbled around a man with a donkey cart. I jogged past a devotee kneeling on a prayer mat. I smiled at a nun. At St Stephen's Gate I wondered: could this really be where St Stephen was stoned? I turned and took a twisting road across the Kidron Valley to the Garden of Gethsemane – then back to the old city wall.

Along the circuit, I passed sites of ancient piety, including the Golden Gate – also known as the Gate of Mercy or the Gate of Eternal Life. I also saw signs of *kitsch* – a bright sign advertising Zedekiah's Cave: only the mouth of it is a natural phenomenon or cave; the interior of the cavern was a quarry carved by slaves and labourers over a period of several thousand years. Mostly the wall around the city is just that, a stone wall – not so different from stone walls surrounding any other old city, I realized. The interest and the joy are inside.

I finally approached New Gate from the opposite direction. Even after detouring to the Garden of Gethsemane, it didn't take as long as I thought it would. It's only two and a half miles around the walls – yet I was sweating. I felt I'd become something more than just a tourist. Somehow exercising and sweating made me feel I belonged to the place – at least momentarily. I think the feeling comes from not just staring at things, trying to work them out, but by being in a place like a resident might, strengthening my body.

Some of the Jerusalem men smiled at me, gave me a thumbs-up. Sometimes other runners grunted a greeting or arched an eyebrow in camaraderie. I was fully part of the Jerusalem scene, and at the same time not quite. This is how we talk about

God's reign: fully here but not quite fully here – proleptic. It is apprehended in flashes, but you are in it all the time. The thought that I was running around Jerusalem's Old City prickled my scalp. With Parry, I was glad: Vivat! Vivat! Vivat!

As Ann and I navigated our way through the city together, I smiled when I saw some of the extraordinary sights. Places of devotion and holiness, like the Cenacle, the Holy Sepulchre, the Noble Sanctuary, the Wailing Wall, moved me deeply. We visited beautiful churches, and the solemn, righteous, galvanizing Yad Vashem, the World Holocaust Remembrance Center[2] ('Never Again!').

Yet the things we encountered weren't all inspiring or salutary: a hideous wall slashes through modern East Jerusalem, separating the Israeli from the Palestinian. Armed young Israeli soldiers are in evidence everywhere. I found their brio frightening, not reassuring. Amid the religious history and pious sentiments there was a hard feeling of uniformed, girded-up military readiness. I wondered if there isn't another way to ensure the safety of the city. Franciscan pacifism would have it so. One day, across the Jaffa Road from the Old City wall, a crowd of shouting students protested about the status quo. I was riled up by the idea of an exclusive homeland at the expense of the Arab population, by the idea of entitlement, by the prevalence of an ideology of protectionism and militarism.

A man accosted me once, demanding in English that I join him in a denunciation of the Palestinians, and sign a petition. When I refused, he cursed me. Because I could feel myself getting hyped up for a no-win fight, I moved on. I felt defensive and offended. I remembered a close Arab family friend whose family had been forced out of Jerusalem in 1948 during the *Nakba*, The Disaster, when the state of Israel was founded, and the Palestinian inhabitants were dispossessed. Because of loyalty to her, I felt some ambivalence about being in Jerusalem. At the same time, I knew I couldn't allow prejudice or hatred to metastasize in my heart. Reaching for some kind of acceptance of these things I could not change, I wondered how in this conflicted situation I could stay grounded and grateful.

Jogging around the city as an individual pilgrim or traveller, I realized I couldn't make much of an impact on the political tensions with which Jerusalem is agog. It would have been magical thinking to believe I could come up with a solution singlehandedly or have done what Francis did. Yet in the recovery movement, people are reminded that just showing up for life is a powerful witness. We have no idea of the impact we have on others, or what might happen because of our presence. Some days it feels nothing happens – other days, who knows?

Often our own story is full of memories of people we never really knew well, but whom we saw week after week at meetings – smiling, listening, being gracious. Their presence was a huge gift – a pledge that the pain and struggle will pay off, that there is something to look forward to. Showing up is crucial to changing the world. Shopkeepers and others often thanked us for being in Jerusalem. Going to Jerusalem was one of the ways I could take a personal part as a 'citizen diplomat' in the Middle East peace process.

I first learned about 'citizen diplomacy' when I went with the Fellowship of Reconciliation to Iran as part of my observance of my 50th birthday. I wanted to do something significant to mark the occasion. When ordinary people meet up across cultural, political, religious divides the results can be eye-opening for all concerned. In terms of social analysis, if one changes the relationship among people at the lowest, most basic, level, it shifts the power structures. In Iran, we had to endure talks with Ayatollahs and clerics, but best of all were the informal conversations we had with students, people on the streets and those in our hotel. They were eager to meet us, friendly, generous.

My group reciprocated. Because we were basically nobodies, we had no burden of speaking for the American people or government. We weren't official representatives. No trade deals, arms reduction talks, no political wrangling, because our power was different. However, in the larger political situation, that visit to Iran complicated my trip to Israel. I had to get a new passport to travel to Israel, because the Iranian visa in my passport would have disqualified me. However, the bureaucracy couldn't take away from our primary purpose in going to Iran or my trip to Israel: we were bearing witness to our common humanity. Seeking ways of reconciliation.

In Jerusalem, the eminent sanity of ordinary people, Jews, Arabs, and others in a wonderfully diverse-looking crowd doing ordinary things, reassured me. Children walked to school with school bags on their backs and greeted me. I watched women shop in the market. Old men sat in cafés, drinking coffee, reading the paper. This is how you live in extraordinary places riven by political and religious passions. I suppose it could all be disrupted in the blink of an eye: the explosion of a suicide bomb, the crack of a rifle, a fog of tear gas. With that perspective, the daily life of Jews and Arabs that I saw in this city is courageous.

I was encouraged by my discovery, in the English-language newspaper, of a lively culture of dissent to what I perceived as the wall-building, gun-toting power politics. Yet the way to experience Jerusalem as a pilgrim seemed to be in being present, mentally, physically and spiritually, to this holy place with my own sword sheathed or – better yet – discarded. Walking around with a sense of grievance or indignation only blinded me to my main reason for visiting Jerusalem, to visit the holy sites. It is a hard-learned skill of diplomats to disagree and keep the channels for conversation open, seeking areas of agreement for fruitful dialogue. Repeatedly razed and re-built, Jerusalem has been the site of horrendous human pain for thousands of years. It is the place of crucifixion. Yet still, it is the City of David shining on the hill and the place of resurrection.

Being one who prefers straightforward situations, the spiritual challenge to me has always been my struggle to live with ambiguity and tension. My life is marked with my failures – and occasional successes – at holding two ideas in my head and heart at once, embracing comprehension rather than single-mindedness. In community life, two brothers can disagree, and both be right. I tend towards good versus bad, right versus wrong. Jerusalem gave me a chance to reflect on the beauty of 'both/and', instead of 'either/or'.

In Jerusalem or Israel nothing ever seems to be simple or straightforward. Because it is one of the great pilgrimage sites of the world, everything that happens there is magnified many times over. The city is the historical omphalos of three religions. David, Jesus, Mohammed, and countless others have left their footprints there. Pilgrims and saints have invested the place with their hopes and fears.

For Jews, it is the subject of the Passover cry: 'Next year in Jerusalem!' And at the Wailing Wall they unburden their hearts. Christians want to follow the Way of the Cross and pray in the Holy Sepulchre. For Muslims, with Mohammad's ascent to heaven from the Noble Sanctuary or Haram al-Sharif, the city is a celestial portal, or at least a window into the divine, second only to Mecca.

For all of these People of the Book, Jerusalem has held a promise of insight or encounter with God, a deepening of faith and identity. You hear people confess: 'I did thus and such, I went to Jerusalem, and now my life is …' Charles de Foucauld, the great Christian mystic and saint who was a pioneer of modern eremitical spirituality, went on pilgrimage to Jerusalem in 1887 and shortly afterwards joined the Trappists. Later, he went to live in the African desert.

Because of my friendship with Ann, I was better able to negotiate Jerusalem with confidence, patience and a sense of humour. Once, we were picked up by a man who wanted to 'guide' us around. He acted in a friendly manner until, in a narrow street, he turned to us and demanded money. Drawing herself up, Ann said 'Certainly not!' and dismissed him. As we walked away, I felt rattled, but she observed it happens everywhere there are large groups of tourists, all over the world. She shrugged it off. It was harder for me, but when I acknowledged that these were the realities of human life everywhere, and that I have the skills to learn how to work through them, then my belly unclenched. I had a spiritual toehold.

I felt like I'd been in this spiritual territory of fear, anxiety and unknowing many times before. This Jerusalem visit was the apotheosis of the many searching 'pilgrimages' I'd taken on the labyrinth in our backyard out on Long Island, in New York. You don't have to go a long way to travel a spiritual route, though travel can undeniably be a powerful experience. Different strands of my life were coming together during this visit. I have spent many hours talking about pilgrimage as a way to approach a labyrinth, because the goals of a pilgrimage are helpful in exploring the possibilities of a labyrinth walk. My backyard expertise was now crucial to interpreting my time in Jerusalem. Flipping the metaphor, this pilgrimage became a meta labyrinth walk.

As I explained to visitors at the friary, the labyrinth's popularity grew during the Middle Ages. By the eighteenth century there is evidence that pilgrims to various labyrinths in the great cathedrals, like Chartres, had imbued these places with the spiritual significance of Jerusalem's holy sites, and the term *chemin de Jerusalem* was used for labyrinths (Matthews, *Mazes and Labyrinths*, p. 80). The labyrinth does not provide answers to life's problems, any more than an expensive trip to the Holy Land. Nevertheless, for many modern labyrinth walkers and pilgrims, such experiences are useful to discover, or recover, insights and memories. If I walk the labyrinth or travel the world in a distracted state, I will get little out of it. If I calm myself, pay attention to my feet 'kissing the earth', as Thich Nhat Hanh says (*Peace is Every Step*, p. 28), paying attention to my breath and heartbeat, there is often a sense of discovery wherever I find myself.

I became fascinated with labyrinths after experiencing a labyrinth walk as part of a workshop in St Louis, Missouri, in

1998. Encountering the outdoor path unexpectedly, I wandered the pattern uncomprehendingly. I was mildly frustrated at how it kept veering away from and around the centre. These feelings opened a way for other memories of frustration, of missing the centre, of failure, to come to mind. Unsurprising to me now as I review that time, most of my memories were resentments that were alcohol-related. I had not yet had the moment of clarity, the insight to my troubles that would come a year later.

Later, I recognized that part of the way the labyrinth 'works' is the same for me as when I run, noticing feelings, experiencing them, letting them go. Running roads and walking the labyrinth are parallel practices. After entering the labyrinth and starting to follow the path, one begins a process of noticing the thoughts, feelings and memories that get kicked up by association with the twists and turns, impressions that flit across the mind.

When I got to the middle of my first labyrinth I was relieved, elated even. In the middle, the second part of the walk, is the liturgical place of enlightenment. I say 'liturgical' because transformation and enlightenment are what the centre represents, but the experience cannot be forced or engineered in any way. Enlightenment, transformation and insight come at any time. But with mind and heart honoured with attention and awareness, a moment of peace or acceptance is often available at the centre of the labyrinth, just as it is at various times in life.

One of my greatest moments of healing insight at a time of turmoil came while I hung wet clothes on a line. Even though nothing else was happening, I suddenly knew I was going to be all right. Or perhaps the sheer ordinariness of the activity reassured me that the ordinary, true part of me will endure no matter the circumstances. I believe every human being has such moments and can build a beautiful life out of them if they do not smother the transforming moment with drugs, alcohol, or any other compulsive activity.

Walking back out from my first labyrinth experience, I was tempted to leap over the paths and just abandon it, but I kept with it and got a sense of completion. The walk out from the centre, the third part of the walk, is the walk of integration. Here body, mind and spirit face the 'so what?' test 'So, what was the point of that?' One might well ask that after walking a labyrinth, or taking a trip to Jerusalem, running a marathon or bushwhacking through the jungle or climbing to a mountaintop. Questions like these can draw a pilgrim into a reflective frame of mind that is necessary to name spiritual experience and embrace the change it often implies. Some of these are small, like honouring the impulse that inspired me to take 20 minutes to calm down and walk the labyrinth – a significant choice in a busy life. Others are larger: awareness of addiction, or resolve to reconcile a broken relationship, for instance.[3]

A feature of the labyrinth that I value tremendously, and one that stood me in good stead as I wandered around Jerusalem, is that you can trust the pattern. You cannot get lost in a labyrinth as you can in a maze. Likewise, whatever happens, including getting to the labyrinth and going home, is part of the pilgrimage: getting lost, sick or robbed, for instance. Chaucer's *Canterbury Tales* include all sorts of trials as the pilgrims make their way to Canterbury. The conmen and street fighters in Jerusalem became aspects of the trip, not the spoliation of it. Perhaps it is only on the treacherous, tricky pilgrimage, away from our home comforts and the protection of routine, confronted by different, strange or confounding circumstances, that we are finally able to see ourselves in new ways. Perhaps as God sees us: beautiful, frail, dependent, courageous, carrying private burdens of guilt and shame, and incalculable gifts of humour, intelligence and strength.

With my imagination primed for a pilgrimage experience of some significance, one day I determined I would visit the Holy Sepulchre – the place I think of as the centre of Jerusalem and the object of my religious quest: the place of resurrection. At first, I had been deterred by the crowds, then aggrieved by the advice to go at 6 a.m. to avoid them. Finally, I decided the crowds were important. Their noise and smells, the grievous delays and tussle, the unavoidable tiredness, was exactly the point: God and humanity mingling, coming together, making human life holy. Holiness is not just majestic liturgies or serene gardens, but the whole roiling mess of life. Everything is holy.

Jogging along, I feared I'd got lost in old Jerusalem, but the labyrinthian reliability held. I wasn't lost. I found an approach to the Church of the Holy Sepulchre. You twist and turn on the labyrinth, then suddenly you are in the centre. Ducking beneath a display of handbags hanging in front of a stall, twisting through an archway of stone, I found myself in an open plaza paved with large stones of different sizes. There it was. Accustomed to skyscrapers and the Cathedral of St John the Divine in New York, the Church of the Holy Sepulchre seemed small. Inside, however, it is cavernous, dusty, covered with the patina of age.

I queued up at the Tomb with some holy-rollers behind me singing 'Amazing Grace'. Ahead of me a larger squadron of Orthodox pilgrims chanted psalms in a Slavic language. A small group of Filipina nuns embedded in the line were saying their rosary. I decided I would simply breathe in and out. In multilingual Babel-like situations, I can barely remember English, let alone focus myself enough to say any prayers – but if prayer is attentive openness to God, I was praying.

As predicted, it was a long wait, which gave me ample time to gawk at the dark church. All around me were oil lamps. Windows high above permitted a thin light, dim as glow worms. Anywhere that people could touch the surfaces of stone, the stone was worn smooth, scooped out by devotion. The holy tomb itself is encased by scaffolding to hold it together – at least, that is what it looked like. A guide pointed out where a pillar has cracked. The earth has trembled over the years and the ground has settled. The larger church was throbbing with the noise of people singing, praying, exclaiming, weeping – hearts thudded in hundreds of breasts, breath being caught and released. I listened to it all like a country bumpkin at the opera: the Spirit whistled among us.

Eventually, I got to the small Chapel of the Angel that leads to the opening into the Tomb. Several people scuttled from the hole in the wall, and a severe-looking, long-bearded priest indicated I should crawl in there. I did so, with two Filipina nuns pushing in behind me. It's too small to stand in comfortably, so we knelt.

The air was heavy and warm from the accumulated exhalations of all the people who'd arrived there before us. Immediately I began to feel claustrophobic. The nuns stretched out over the sarcophagus, weeping and praying volubly. If I had had more nerve, I would have pointed out that Christ is risen, he is not here! But instead I began to pray fiercely for deliverance.

By the time we scrambled out, I was in a full sweat, a little shaky. Somehow, it became easier to receive the experience of the women who first came to this tomb over 2,000 years ago. Eugene Peterson nails it in *The Message*: 'They got out as fast as they could, beside themselves, their heads swimming. Stunned, they said nothing to anyone' (Mark 16.8).

Because I'd started at the tomb, I toured the church against the flow of pilgrims following Jesus' crucifixion and death. My next stop was the place of the crucifixion. Here, there is a small hole in the stone, the right size for a post. We were encouraged to put our hands in there, rather like St Thomas being told to place his fingers in the wounds of Christ. I put my hand in the place where they erected the cross. It's lined with silver now. It is an example of the impulse to make beautiful what we hold sacred, even such a terrifying location as this.

Later, I asked an English-speaking brother: is that really Golgotha? I thought it would be on the edge of town. Patiently, he affirmed it was. The city walls had moved, but definitely this was the place.

Deep beneath the Holy Sepulchre, in a tenebrous nook off the 29 steps that go down to St Helena's Chapel, I found a quiet space to sit, collect myself, and pray. Recently, my confessor had given me the whole of Psalm 119 as a penance and I'd been stymied by the apparent tediousness of it and wondering at the gravity of my sins that deserved it. The psalm is long! There are 176 verses. As yet, getting through the whole psalm had proved too time-consuming, too easily put off until another time. It was the top priority for Jerusalem. On and on the psalm reads: 'Teach me your commandments', 'I love the way of your commandments', 'Your commandments are dearer to me than gold and silver'. And significantly: 'I will run the way of your commandments, for you have set my heart at liberty' (Psalm 119.32, *The Daily Office SSF*).

Suddenly, I laughed at my confessor's wit. There was nothing to fear in all this; it is a celebration of Scripture, of the loving, gentle ways of God, an invitation to claim the love I feel, and to inhabit the interstices of prayer and service, love and devotion more boldly. Halfway through the psalm, a flash illumined my prayer corner and I looked up to see a boy of about 12 or 13, leaning towards me like people do when they are trying to photograph creatures encountered in the wild. Obviously, he was trying not to disturb me, but wanted the perfect shot: a monk praying in the Holy Sepulchre! When I looked up, he looked embarrassed, and waved at me awkwardly and tip-toed away. Bless his heart. I'd been caught *in flagrante delicto* praying at the centre of my spiritual labyrinth.

On the way back to the monastery I felt light-hearted. The fruits and vegetables in the market seemed to pulse with vivid colours and powerful scents – alive with splendour. Every Friday afternoon, the Roman Catholic Franciscans pray the Way of the Cross, following the traditional Via Dolorosa. Young brothers with a portable sound system struggle and sweat through the streets. I went with the crowd on a couple of occasions, so the stories of Jesus' arrest and death stayed starkly in my mind. I tried, as many do, to follow as best I could the events of Jesus' last hours, the night before his death. /

One of the places I visited on my own that had an unexpected cachet for me was the Garden of Gethsemane. It was the site of Judas' betraying kiss and Jesus' arrest. Lingering among the twisted millennia-old olive trees, I wished they would speak to me. My guide said several were old enough to have sheltered Jesus as he knelt in prayer. I found these massive, gnarled trunks more moving than many of the churches.

I was reminded of a retreat at a monastery in Southern California during my novitiate, when I was feeling angry and fed up with religious life. I'd decided to run away, planning to defect one evening. I secreted a few important documents in my bag and took my uncle's phone number. He lived in the same town as the monastery. I was too afraid to tell the brothers directly I was leaving; I was ashamed it had come to this.

On my chosen evening, I was sidling through the darkened reception room of the monastery when I heard a voice ask: 'Where are you going?' Swallowing my heart, I peered around. I finally spied the oldest brother of our community who had come on retreat too. I confessed my plans and burst into tears. He was quiet for a long time and then told me stories about his early years, admitting that, even now at his age, he had fantasies of leaving on some unbearable days. 'So, I keep a little bag packed,' he said, 'to be ready. But when I want to go, I say to myself: "tomorrow".' He smiled and patted my knee.

The next day I woke early and went on a walk in the hills. At one point, I came across two trees, one very old, gnarled and riven by lightning. Another close by was a sapling. Saplings aren't interesting nor nearly as beautiful as trees that have weathered storms. I decided to wait and see, not to leave just yet.

Running around Jerusalem, reading books about the city, praying at the holy sites in Jerusalem, I came back over and over to a deeper search inside myself. After I got over the nervous literalism ('Did such-and-such really happen here?'), the next layer of inquiry was to take the juxtapositions of time and place as a window into human life. The novel sights and impressions posed questions. 'How do I love you, Lord? What am I doing?' Fear and betrayal have been part of the disciples' story from the beginning. Fortunately, I have a broader experience of discipleship than the *via negativa*. Nevertheless, the more I have learned and experienced, the more certain I am that the truly big picture is beyond me. Like the blind Indians experiencing their part of the elephant, I can only know in part. At the resurrection, I will know fully.

Repeatedly I was impressed by the generosity of Jerusalemites and the vigorous commitment to living fully amid so many uncertainties. Two famous men from Jerusalem, who live in London, Yotam Ottolenghi and Sami Tamimi, authors of the cookbook *Jerusalem*, are a case in point. They ground their hopes for a peaceable future in the most ordinary and important of human activities: eating.

These are gay men, one from a Jewish family, the other from an Arab Palestinian family. Their relationship as friends and business partners, as well as their social vision and culinary manifesto, is an example of the life-giving, socially redeeming gifts the world needs more of. Their recipes point to a primal way of meeting – at the table – with sympathetic understanding and celebration. I read a lot into their gay identity as the reason for their creative non-conformity to the Middle East standoff between Israelis and Palestinians, but I don't even know them.

Jane Kramer wrote in her profile of Yotam Ottolenghi in *The New Yorker* magazine:

Jerusalem includes his nimble, often eloquent evocations of the city and of the helplessness both he and Tamimi feel as 'that elusive dream of peace in the Middle East' fades. He put it this way: 'It takes a great leap of faith, but we are happy to take it – what have we got to lose? – to imagine that hummus will eventually bring Jerusalemites together, if nothing else will.'
('The Philosopher Chef', 3 December 2012)

It's the perfect gesture of faith. Through friendship, sharing food, and working together we are all confronted with the possibilities for God's redeeming work in and through all creation. Hummus doesn't have sectarian religious baggage, though there are contentious discussions about the origins of hummus. Ottolenghi writes: ' … when push comes to shove, nobody seriously challenges the Palestinian hegemony in making hummus, even though both they and the Jews like calling it their own …' (Ottolenghi and Tamimi, *Jerusalem*, p. 112).

The visit to Jerusalem reminded me that in a bewildering time, full of uncertainty, war, and incendiary passions, by pursuing ordinary activities fearlessly, humorously and with a sense of shared humanity, we are being the kind of people God wants us to be, doing the kind of work God wants us to do. By jogging, if you will, along the path of our life, using whatever tools and resources – like the labyrinth – or chances to travel if they come our way, we can learn from, and let go of, the different experiences we carry in our hearts and bodies. These are the disciplines that can prepare us for that moment of clarity or understanding that will enable us to engage with our times with real strength and bravery when necessary, as well as more generously, gently, generatively.

I am eager to see dividing walls come tumbling down, hearts inflamed with love, friendships forged, and community created. The philosopher chef's speculations about the reconciling potential of hummus made me hungry for it. Cooking being my oldest passion - I've cooked since I was eleven - I developed a version I can prepare on the run, so to speak. Hummus is an extremely simple food to prepare. Here is what the food editior of the *New York Times* calls a no-recipe recipe for a runner's hummus.

Set up your food processor with the steel blade and dump into it a can of chickpeas that have been rinsed. Throw in some garlic, as much as you like, though I advise a light touch because part of the pleasure of hummus is the sweet, nutty flavour of the beans and tahin.

Next, add a tablespoon of tahini. Sometimes when we don't have any – friary kitchens often contain only very basic foods – I have been known to use a dollop of creamy organic peanut butter. I love peanut butter and could happily eat it on anything, though it may not contribute to peace in the Middle East! Squeeze in some lemon juice and turn on the food processor. Let it go until the hummus is silky smooth. You may need to add more lemon juice or cold water to get it smooth enough. Taste it before adding salt and pepper.

If you are feeling adventurous and happen to have some around, a few pieces of roasted pepper or perhaps some avocado thrown in give the hummus extra interest. Live boldly! Invite your friends to have some too.

Eat it with a spoon, scoop it up with a celery stalk, smear it on some whole wheat bread, or if you are lucky eat it with pita bread. We almost never have any in the pantry. A small portion of this amazing power food settles comfortably in my stomach and I feel energized for my run and ready to engage the world.

Notes

1 'Franciscans and the Holy Land: Interview with Vicar of Custody, 13th March 2005', *Zenit*, Available at: https://zenit.org/articles:franciscans-and-the-holy-land (accessed 8.12.18)

2 See www.yadvashem.org (accessed 11.4.19)

3 For more information about labyrinths, see the work of the Revd Lauren Artress and Veriditas. Available at: https://www.veriditas.org (accessed 11.4.19). I am indebted to her pioneering work.

10

Foiling fear and experiencing healing in community: Grahamstown, South Africa

Who we are can only be understood in its biggest sense not its smallest sense. It is our bodies, our actions and our thoughts, our relationships together in and with Christ, our lives in the Spirit that all make up the 'real' me – or more accurately the real 'us'. True identity for Paul is to be found not in the 'me-ness of me' but in the 'us-ness of us'. (Gooder, *Body*, p. 102)

The brothers of the Episcopalian Order of the Holy Cross live at Mariya uMama weThemba Monastery, a modest monastery in Grahamstown, South Africa. They invited me to come for a time of rest and rejuvenation – a mini-sabbatical at Christmas 2013 – in the midst of engagements in Istanbul, Jerusalem, and Honiara in the Solomon Islands. The Eastern Cape location is rugged, filled with farms and forests, craggy escarpments, and fields of broken stones and scrubby brush. Their home, a cluster of multi-hued brick buildings, with a campanile next to the chapel, is nestled in a nook of the hills, protected from the winds that bluster over the Eastern Cape. They have a view peering down a steep hillside. The large chapel window frames mostly sky. Native plants push up through the scree; non-native plants are scrupulously uprooted. It's the kind of place where you think monks and hermits might like to live. The horizon of ever-receding hills is framed by rocky ridges in the foreground. You reach the monastery by a dirt road that branches off the main paved road. It is the back of beyond.

I think of the monks of the Order of the Holy Cross as cousins to us Franciscans. As Episcopalians, neither Order is large; I find something deeply compatible in their generous, compassionate, friendly way of living the religious life. There is a long history of friendship between the two Orders. Several of the brothers have been of particular help to me over the years.

Slipping out of a side door of the monastery one December day, I headed up the steep dirt drive for a run. On my right the ground dropped away, there was a vegetable garden near the road, then pastureland falling precipitously to the bottom of a valley – or perhaps 'ravine' would be a better name for the small, deep cleft in the hills. At the bottom are several large plastic tanks, storing spring water that is pumped to the top of the hill behind the monastery, from where it flows down into the houses. I find their water strategies intriguing – so different from being connected to water mains.

At the top of the drive is the Holy Cross School. The brothers built the school for the local children. The school is for the first three years of schooling, and the idea is to help the children develop the academic and social skills they need to do well in the next levels of school. All the children come from the rural area around the monastery. I heard heartbreaking stories of family difficulties: violence, alcoholism, abuse. But I also heard equally poignant stories about sacrifice, dignity, and determination to help the children succeed. As I ran past the school to the head of the driveway leading to the dirt road that runs past the property, the children saw me and shouted and waved. They ran to the fence surrounding their schoolyard. I waved and shouted back to them. Once I was taken to visit the school by one of the brothers. Several tiny boys wearing red sweaters clustered around my knees, clamouring for my attention. One climbed me as if I were a tree, grabbing around my neck with both arms. 'Hello! Hello!' he shouted. 'How are you? I love you!'– trying out all the English phrases he knew. A messenger from God. Sometimes nothing matters so much as being present to one another. Fancy words, clever insights, all melt away in a child's eager, primal hug.

Almost every day I ran past the schoolyard, then through farms and open countryside. My route along the dust-choked road took me 4 miles to a concrete communications tower. I slapped the gate posts there as a signpost to myself, and then returned to the monastery. Pine and gum trees grew alongside the road. In places, the trees had been logged; charred wood was evidence that fire had swept over the landscape. As I went along, I followed grass pastures, fence lines – in the distance were farmsteads and irrigation ponds. I stomped through dry, rocky land, checking where cattle and other animals foraged. While I never got a clear idea about what a springbok looked like, or any of the other wild antelope, whatever it was I saw, some of them definitely weren't cows.

The road meandered, looping over an old train track. I could see where what looked like fuelling stations had been, water tanks. Often, I passed men loading firewood into a cart pulled by a pair of donkeys. Sometimes when I passed by the men nodded and smiled; other times they seemed more guarded or preoccupied with gathering the wood. I became unremarkable. At one farm, large Dobermans snarled and raced towards me once or twice, making me queasy with anxiety every time I ran by; their hullabaloo roused the farmer to shout alpha commands, and he brought them to heel. I wasn't bitten, although it felt like a test of faith to pass that way.

'Watch out for the baboons!' the brothers cautioned. 'If you see one, don't stare at it. Don't make quick movements. Sometimes they attack.' This warning put me on hyper-alert for several days. I thought I saw baboons among the pine trees or sitting on the eucalyptus stumps. But these turned out to be nothing, or cows or some other kind of large creature. Eventually, the absence of baboons made me forget them.

One day, I crossed the old railway tracks, and was heading up towards a gate that led on to a track leading down to a reservoir. It was foggy. Summers in the Eastern Cape are not so different from summers – or winters – in Snohomish, Washington State, where I grew up. My feet pock-pock-pocked on the gravel. I was breathing rhythmically, inhaling the brain-clearing, heart-enlarging pine-scented oxygen. Every once in a while, my conditioning and the environmental conditions are in alignment and I run with particular ease, freely. Skimming the road, oblivious to anything except a kind of thoughtless wellbeing, my eyes were half-focused, as in meditation. The baboon took me by surprise. He – or she – was seated in the middle of the road, watching me alertly. Its dog-like face and primate body are distinctive. Some baboons have large ruffs of hair, but this one had a buzz-cut toughness about him.

When I finally registered the animal's presence and recalled my friends' warnings, I stopped in alarm. A spasm tightened my chest. I could feel my balls contracting and panic rising in my throat. Realizing I was wearing a red cap, I pulled it off slowly. Maybe baboons would be antagonized by red, I thought, in the same way that I'd heard that bulls charge at red things. What did I know? I was operating on fear and conjecture. Hiding the cap under my arm, I looked away, trying to gauge my chances against the animal.

Not good, I decided. If it took it into its head to grab my cap, or to attack me for any other reason, I would be too slow and too weak. My heart hammered, and a cold, greasy sweat broke out on my chest. I turned to sidle away. Then I realized I was surrounded by baboons. I'd blundered into a troop. Some were sitting on fence posts alongside the road, others were walking along, not paying me any attention. But several of them seemed to be staring at me – with rapt attention.

I've been mugged by human beings a couple of times. Each time there was a sense of menacing nonchalance with hard stares that preceded the attack. I tried to placate these creatures.

'Sorry,' I muttered. 'Now, now,' I babbled. I didn't want to stare provocatively, nor was I comfortable turning my back on the troop of them, so I crab-walked, balling up my red cap, faking calmness even as I was thinking they might sense my distress and seize their advantage. They watched me intently. I walked slowly and deliberately for 25 yards or so, until I decided they had no interest in me. Cautiously I started to jog, then when they continued to do nothing, I sprinted out of there, running as fast as I possibly could.

Thinking back on it, I'm not sure if it was a narrow escape or not. But I wonder what they saw? Was I a threat to them? Baboons move in groups for safety. Since my encounter, I've read a bit about them and know that they have a social life. These were members of the Chacma breed of baboon, common to the Eastern Cape. Running back to the monastery – returning to my troop for safety – I realized I'm not so different from them. I felt relief to be safe with the brothers in the monastery. But at the same time, I wondered at the chance I'd had to be like St Francis. The possibility that wild baboons can understand human speech is nil – especially to follow an argument. But that didn't stop Francis. Why shouldn't I reach out to them too, I wondered. What would I say to them? 'Peace, sisters and brothers!' Francis always claimed kinship with people, creatures, different features of nature. But my fear and impatience overwhelmed any idea of kinship exploration that December morning. However, with patience and some education about other species, in this case Chacma baboons, it must be possible to enter more fully into the workings of their minds. As Elizabeth Marshall Thomas, the author of *The Hidden Life of Dogs*, has written: 'When we relegate animal thought to instinct, we overlook the fact that instinct is merely an elegant matrix for the formation of an intellect, a fail-safe device that guides each species to form thoughts. When shaped by education, our thoughts enable us to do what we do, and even to be what we are, not only as members of our species but as individuals' (p. viii). What were these baboons thinking as they stared at me?

Toying with the idea of a Christmas sermon to the baboons, I did some reading about them and discovered an extraordinary story of a radical change within a troop in Kenya. They weren't Chacmas, however. Another difference is that male Chacmas are not known for their close relationships with other baboons, female or male, Chacmas or otherwise. But the differences didn't obscure some intriguing possibilities. The idea that other animals think and can communicate ideas to one another has been observed and documented in a report on some Kenyan baboons by Dr Robert M. Sapolsky, a professor of biology and neurology at Stanford, and his wife, Dr Lisa J. Share. I read in *The New York Times* of their observations about the changes in a troop of baboons he calls 'The Forest Troop'. They learned to live peacefully and adopted uncharacteristic behaviours which they taught to newcomers (Angier, 'No Time for Bullies' 13 April 2004). It is challenging to think about a troop of baboons embracing a way of life held so casually and perhaps contemptuously by so many human beings. I was reminded of St Paul's suggestion in his letter to the Colossians that the good news of God is not for humans alone, but for 'every creature under heaven' (Colossians 1.23).

I have my sermon. If I have another chance, I'm ready!

Squatting to minimize an aggressive stance, I smack my lips as a sign of affection and friendship.

Palms open to show non-aggression, I speak in a gentle voice:

A Christmas Homily to the Chacma Baboons

Merry Christmas to you! Merry Christmas to you! I am celebrating the birth of Jesus Christ with a cross-species initiative here. I know you could tear me apart. But so far so good, yes? I'm taking this risk because God took a risk on the world a long time ago. He decided to become part of it. He came naturally, born of a human mother. And after 33 years he got torn apart: ripped to shreds by my own species. But that wasn't the end of the story. He rose from the dead, and immediately started preaching peace. What do you do when surrounded by a pack of enemies, fierce as wolves, howling for blood? Well, bravely, he started talking about peace.

His modus operandi was to sit down with some like-minded folks, his disciples. Not that any of them were perfect. They'd shown their weaknesses – running away at his hour of need, competing for power and privilege in his little group of disciples. They complained. They only seemed to half-listen to him sometimes. But they were the ones he had to work with, just ordinary people. He wanted ordinary people in his troop, because that is how our God has always worked – through ordinary folks showing up the proud, the strong, and the great who, for all their perks and privileges, can generally be relied on to take the world down a long low road of war, competition, lies, murder and corruption of every kind.

Which brings me to you. My first point is: be happy! Give thanks. You and I know you are just regular baboons. But, as I'm saying, that's a plus! There is something beautiful about just being a baboon, just being who you are, you know? My word to you right now is: Bless you!

You are the glory of God in your beauty, your aliveness, your baboonish ways. God gave you the ability to run, something I like to do too, but I must admit you are so much better at it than I am.

You've been clocked at 35 miles per hour. Didn't know that, did you? A real blessing when it comes to foraging, survival. And speaking from my 8 miles per hour point of view: astounding joy to move like that! I don't complain about my slowness, I'm just glad to be alive, to be able to move and enjoy the beauty all around me.

As my second point, I want to start off with a confession. Human beings are hopeless at peace. We fight, we quarrel, we kill: I'm not standing above you. I'm not disrespecting you as much as mourning the failures of my species. While all of us humans have violent impulses – we feel anger, hate and all of that – at the same time many of us try to live differently. We have developed strategies that some, not all, have found to be helpful. We talk, we try to find projects to do together, we – sometimes – share our wealth, so that poor folks with a good reason to be angry can share in the blessings.

Some of us stand by prayer as a great way to break through to a new consciousness. Then we look out for ways to meet up with people in pain and grief and suffering and we try to share with them, sometimes just sit or walk with them. We look for ways to help others. Sounds nice, yes? But then somebody gets ticked off and we seem to end up back at square one.

Our work is to dig deep into the heart and not to lose hope. That's why these celebrations like Christmas are so important – they remind us of what we can be when we cooperate with God.

What does all this have to do with you? Well, the evidence shows you guys are capable of learning things. There is a troop of baboons – let's call them your cousins – up in Kenya who have started to live peacefully. They've turned away from infanticide, they no longer attack and kill others just for fun or sex or even territory. And they have done some real gender-bending, role-warping experimentation with the family values thing.

The big change started when all the alpha males died off after eating contaminated meat. Being typical snarly toughs, they fought off everybody else and ate a pile of bad meat. And then got sick and died. Couldn't have happened to nicer guys. The ones who didn't taste the meat or drink the Kool-Aid survived, and they decided that was it with the tough-guy way of running things. Probably they all felt just a little bit relieved those guys were out of the picture, because they started to loosen things up and show their true colours.

The women started looking around for help with the kids. And those sweet uncles – you know the ones – the subordinate, quiet guys who don't like to fight, who hang out with their special friends, and don't seem to have much interest in the girls. Okay, I might be over-identifying here, and reading more into their story than I should – but I'm making a bigger point with you guys: well, they started to help with the child care.

Once they got involved with that, everybody started thinking: every life is precious. Those boys started to get some confidence and they all came together and started to live without all the fighting and macho show-off behaviour. Though when there was danger, these guys surprised everybody, they teamed up and fought off any bad-ass who tried to spoil the situation. Then, they took it to the next level; they found ways to allow new guys into the group, but they made them sign up to a new customary, peaceful behaviour.

Are you tired of seeing your kids killed off, just so some alpha male can get his rocks off?[1]

You ever wonder if there isn't a way to welcome strangers that's different from bared teeth and lunging for the jugular?

God has blessed every community with the resources they need to flourish. Ordinary, down-to-earth folks have got what it takes; God has bet everything on folks just like us – because none of us is all that special from a worldly way of thinking. But a godly perspective gives ultimate value and importance to everything that lives and moves and has its being here on the planet earth. It means listening to everybody, even the same-sex loving, fight-hating brothers and sisters who you may never have given much thought to. And to you boys and girls in the back row there, it also means you can't hide your brilliance, you've got to let it shine!

If they can do it in Kenya, you can do it down here on the Cape. A change in your lives could mean a radical change in the lives of others. Not least, of course, a great example for my fellow humans. We are looking for ways to become better animals.

Sing it out: 'Glory to God in the highest!' Let all the earth rejoice and sing. A new day is coming, and all of us need to play our parts. Be full of joy and peace.

Amen.

The astounding facts unearthed by Dr Sapolsky and his wife Dr Share in their research on the Kenyan baboons make me wistful. The question arises: if baboons can do it, why can't we humans? Of course, there are many people who adapt to change, learn new, peaceful behaviours, and communicate them effectively to others. Yet humans struggle to consolidate their so-called advanced society. The life-giving, peace-promoting, justice-based initiatives that give birth to a higher civilization emerge and fall back. We humans love our wars and military victories. We are susceptible to thinking 'might makes right' and we boast of superpower status and the moral high ground. In many places around the world the contributions of same-sex loving men and women are often discredited or lost altogether. What are we afraid of?

One of the things about the hope for a transformation of consciousness, a Great Awakening of the Spirit of love, compassion and justice, is that we need to learn to work with fear (Richo, *When the Past is Present*, p. 94). Awareness of fear, acceptance of it, can give birth to different things. God-fearing caution, for instance, not taking crazy chances. We need to embrace that. Fear can also move us quickly out of harm's way. By the same token it can lead to courage. Courage is fear that has said its prayers, I once read. Everybody experiences fear, but not everybody is governed by it, in my experience. When I feel rattled before preaching or when I feel a knot in my stomach as I open a meeting, I ask myself what is it that I am afraid of. Facing fear means I can smile, I can use humour, I can trust that the preparation and the guidance of the Holy Spirit have equipped me for the moment. In recovery, I've heard people say: 'God didn't bring you this far just to drop you on your bum.' That's a typical, earthy and cogent observation from a group of folks who know more than most about what fear can do in your life.

When I did my inventory of my faults and shortcomings in early sobriety, I was asked to look at the motivation behind my transgressions. Over and over I identified fear: afraid of being left out made me aggressive, afraid of my security being transgressed made me defensive and prone to saying harsh, dismissive things, and fear of being considered a loser made me do all kinds of things. Alcohol eroded any sense of restraint, so that I lashed out verbally, thinking I was standing up for myself. I ignored the boundaries people put in place around themselves, saying I was just showing them love. I was afraid nobody would or could love me, so I tried to grab what I could get.

After I had been sober for seven or eight years, a friend once asked me what would happen if I now had a drink. 'A drink?' I asked. 'Nothing with just one, except the desire to have another and then another. After three or four,' I told him, 'all bets are off. I might try to kiss you. Or maybe punch you. It all depends on whether I'm angry or feeling amorous. If I remember right, I could go from amorous to pissed off in the blink of an eye.' He quickly offered to buy me another Coca-Cola. Now I use the fearful feeling to pray, to reach out peacefully to others, respectful of boundaries, and I give thanks for what my life is about.

There is a popular story about St Francis confronting a wolf. It might be more fable than news account, but the story is provocative in its ability to engage the imagination. The townspeople of Gubbio were in paroxysms of fear because a wolf was threatening their flocks. Some even feared for the safety of their families. When Francis arrived, he told the people to stay in town while he went with his companion to the forest. There he met the wolf that had been troubling them. 'Peace, Brother Wolf!' he said. Francis and the wolf struck a deal. If the wolf promised not to attack the sheep and people of Gubbio, then Francis would ask them to feed him. With this pact between them made, Francis and the animal returned to the town where Francis announced the deal. And the people agreed to it. They fed the wolf, and it lived among them, and was a vivid reminder of the visit of St Francis. Franciscan preachers have used this story in many ways. It is part of the reason Francis is often portrayed with a wolf at his side and a dove on his shoulder. For me it is an example of profound empathy, of Francis demonstrating his understanding of the wolf's situation.

Interpreting or appropriating the story also raises the question of feeding the inner wolf. Am I willing to take on the burden of caring for my wolf? In other words, am I willing to care for the fierce part of myself, so that the destructive energy transforms into something else? Protective, perhaps? Or a creative collaboration I've not yet dreamed of?

Running is one way I feed the wolf. I burn off excess energy, and I focus my anger and frustration into physical goals of ticking off the miles. As I feel the strength in my body I am aware of my strength and the power I have for good and evil. Part of what keeps me sober is the use of prayer to take me deep into the wounds and hungers in me, and the blessing from new ideas when old issues are held attentively and prayerfully with love and awareness of God's help. Prayer keeps alive the aspiration to be gentle yet strong, vulnerable yet trusting, and always raises the reminder to be grateful for the gifts that have been given to me.

Gratitude is the real product of the transformative power of prayer. Nearly anything can be turned into good, or at least let go of with grace, when I mention it in my prayers with gratitude.

When I'm not happy, or when bad or difficult things happen, I thank God for the help that is expected and implied in every challenge. I can be grateful for the confidence that, as my mother has said, 'If it doesn't kill me, it will make me stronger.'

Running along that country road in South Africa, I was reminded of the extraordinary example of people facing their fear and making a valiant attempt to live differently. With the South African Truth and Reconciliation Commission (TRC), the nation was taken through a process of confronting fear, exhuming and examining the stereotypes and hearsay that fuelled the hateful policy of apartheid. I've watched documentaries of the hearings and read a lot about the TRC. I've watched white men who raped, plundered and killed black people tell the story of what they did, and at the same time through the camera's lens I've watched the faces of the survivors listening to the stories.

One moment particularly stays in my mind. It was the story of a woman whose son had been taken and brutally killed. I remember the anger and indignation rising up in me as I watched – and it took my breath away to hear the old woman weeping and saying through her tears: 'I forgive you!' Later, she said it was such a relief to know what had happened to her son. White soldiers were equally moved by telling their secrets, exposing their guilt and grief over what had happened. Some had been motivated by the desire to serve their country; but they were caught up in a twisted system.

Watching all this was intensely moving. It was like watching angels unshackle them, touching them so that the scales fell from their eyes like riot shields clattering to the ground. Freed. Disarmed. Of course, not all the atrocities were perpetrated by whites on blacks, and the painful, cleansing stories were told by black people too. It is becoming clearer as time goes by that the work of the TRC must be ongoing. The healing of over 400 years of outrageous oppression can't be accomplished quickly.

Another people who faced the demons among them through a Truth and Reconciliation Commission – the people of the Solomon Islands – ended up rejecting guns wholesale. At least they made a grand gesture. At the end of the ethnic tension in that country in 2004 the members of the Anglican religious orders went and collected many guns from the people. Hundreds and hundreds of arms were recovered, then taken in canoes out into the middle of Iron Bottom Sound and pitched overboard, to rust in peace. Such a forthright, no-holds-barred approach. One of the unanticipated consequences of this wholesale disarmament has been an increase in the numbers of crocodiles in the rivers. But the threat of a crocodile attack is less destructive of community cohesion than the horror of seeing dead bodies riddled with bullets and knowing who had done it.

As an American, I wonder when our own racial wounds will be healed. There are many beautiful examples of where this healing work is happening. But the hydra-headed gorgon of racial hatred, of white supremacy, of political gerrymandering and economic oppression still lashes out. When will we approach each other sympathetically, seeking friendship across the divides? When will we reject violence categorically? Do we have the guts to throw our guns into the sea? Do we have the heart to confess our hatred, our political myopia, our racism? Pacifism is never a popular political position, but it is for me the only stance I can hold with integrity as a Franciscan. Francis's admonition to his brothers not to ride horses or to handle money came from his understanding about the connection between money, powerful horses, war, bloodshed and violence. One of the Franciscan concerns today is to try and identify what are the comparable things to avoid in our lives now. Guns, absolutely. No friar should be handling one of those. Pope Francis rejects large cars, preferring to ride in a small, inexpensive car. Franciscans have made sincere commitments to living more lightly and simply on the earth, but it isn't a checklist that is helpful. Rather, attaining comparability with Francis in our day is healing people, healing and restoring the earth, establishing justice and peace on earth to the glory of God.

The Hopi people run as prayer,[2] dedicating their runs for different causes, sometimes for rain or for other people in their community. Getting out and moving along trails, experiencing the wind, sun, rain, heat or cold, sweating, struggling – in some ways this opens them to God. They are vulnerable to God or, as they say, 'the Great Spirit'. As a runner needs help to push through the exhaustion and frailty that comes to each of us, humans need help pushing through the barriers that divide us and prevent us from living lives of grace and beauty. We can't force God to do anything, but by emptying ourselves we can be filled with the God-force. And what about the rain? I've never had any impact on the weather, but I know people who claim to have that connection and power.

When I returned to the monastery from my run, I paused to contemplate the sign at the top of the monastery driveway: *Uxolo*. Peace. We use the term so freely. All around us there are instructive examples of people and animals living differently and embracing peace. Yet wars rage, refugees crowd into boats, children die. A friend has written:

> To be redeemed is to be saved from being stopped or driven by fear or desire. We feel fear and desire as givens of life. Yet, through our trusting there is a meaning in our suffering, we are no longer at the mercy of fear or desire. We can feel afraid and unsatisfied, but not have to be driven or stopped as a result. (Richo, *The Five Things We Cannot Change*, p. 45)

Notes

1 Rhodi Lee, 'Infanticide: Biggest Threat to Baby Chacma Baboons? Adult Males (and here's what females do to prevent it)', *Tech Times*, November 14, 2014.

2 See John McClung, 'Runners You Should Know: The Hopi', *Barefoot in Arizona* (blog) at http://bfinaz.blogspot.com/2012/09/runners-you-should-know-hopi.html (Accessed 26 11.16).

11

Making the dream come true: Half Moon Bay International Marathon, California

Running has taken me in, and continues to comfort, heal and challenge me in all kinds of magical ways. I am not a 'good runner' because I am me. I am a good 'me' because I am a runner. (Armstrong, 'Why I Run', *Runner's World*, 18 October 2006)

Around Christmas 2015 I began to think about running a marathon. Even though this is not so much a book about the sport of cross country running as a testimonial to the spiritual impact of being physically active on my body and soul, I felt this book needed a race story. Also, perhaps, I needed a running credential of some sort. How hard could it be? I wondered. For years, I ran 6 miles three or four times a week. All I'd need to do was gradually increase that, and within six or seven months I'd be ready.

I found a race that fitted into my scheduled time in California. Then, looking on the internet, I found eight-week training schedules, diets that would help build stamina, even exercises that would strengthen my body, augmenting the running. It all sounded tremendously encouraging. But I largely ignored it because in many ways diet was out of my control, especially the fancy-sounding ones they were recommending, and the prospect of going to a gym for 'cross training' was daunting. I decided I'd rely on Cross Prayers instead, meaning praying with arms outstretched. This, I thought, would be easy.

The trouble was, I'd never run farther than 10 or 12 miles, and at Christmas I couldn't even run that far.

But I started. At first it was just increasing the number of days I ran, pushing myself to run five days a week. In January, I travelled to Australia and there I guess-timated I ran 10 miles, once. In the Solomon Islands, with February and March temperatures around 85 to 90 degrees Fahrenheit, my usual 6 or 7 miles was the limit of my endurance. New Zealand, with its cool autumnal April weather, gave me a real boost of energy, and I could push myself to 12 miles, then one day 14 miles. I got back to the friary at Te Ara Hou village, shaking violently and with extremely painful feet. Taking off my shoes, I discovered my socks were soaked with blood. The shoes had worn out and I had blackened toe nails.

In May, with new shoes in Los Angeles, I trailed around parks and city streets, but was unable to find the enthusiasm to run much – too many cars, too much dust. It was depressing. In England during June I ran 14 to 15 miles several times – at least, that is what we conjectured standing around with cups of tea and guessing wildly at the distances from my tales of where I'd gone.

It wasn't until July on holiday with my mother in Snohomish that I ran 18 measured miles for the first time. This emboldened me to register for the Half Moon Bay International Marathon scheduled for September 18. But later that month, when I was in Papua New Guinea and enduring tropical heat, I had a serious setback: one day I ran 9 or 10 miles and keeled over in a dead faint after getting a drink of water from the tank.

I returned to San Francisco with three weeks to push myself in preparation for the marathon on September 18. The first thing I did was run 22 to 23 miles – by my waffle-o-meter – to see if I could come anywhere near the goal of 26.2 miles. Other runners warned me off trying a full distance of the marathon while training, saying it was better to leave something for race day. The first time I ran 23 miles I came home and fell to the floor, shaking and gasping for air. But lodged in the back of my brain was the realization I had just run farther than I'd ever run. That was a red-letter day. For some reason, it never occurred to me that barely managing something once is not the same as being physically fit.

It is important to have dreams, aspirations for life. My running dreams seemed to be of a piece with other ambitions and hopes I nurtured. From dreaming of happiness and following the road of sobriety to achieve it, I knew dreams could be fulfilled too. Even in the face of massive evidence to the contrary, people have continued to dream of freedom, justice, equality, lasting peace. These 'meta-' dreams have their roots in smaller victories, in words of encouragement from elderly mentors, from a burning sense that it is better to try to give than to give in to a bland acceptance of the easiest way through life. Or to allow fear to immobilize us.

Over the months, the dream of running a marathon had taken on a larger significance: I would be staking a claim on a piece of God's dominion. The marathon became a metaphor for everything I hoped my life had been about.

Even more, the marathon became a pledge to myself to follow a trajectory of hard work and determination that could make a difference in the world. It is not that life is like a marathon, but that the desire to push against the negative, no-hope, hold-your-peace attitude that lurked in my mind is the holiest part of me. It is what St Paul calls the 'upward call of God in Jesus Christ'. Where would the world be without the animating dream of St Francis, or Dr King, or Dorothy Day, or Bishop Tutu, or Gandhi? These stalwarts of my personal cloud of witnesses egged me on to dream and to act on it, to give my life to God, to dedicate myself to justice, persevere even when I felt I was failing.

Because of these closely harboured beliefs about the impact of dreams on my life and vocation, running a marathon infiltrated my prayers. It seemed that I was surrounded by stories of people who faced huge odds, both voluntarily and through the crash of evil circumstances, but who found a way to create something good and beautiful. In July, I learned about the team of refugees competing in the Olympics. I used them as my guiding stars. They competed 'for dignity', as S. L. Price wrote in *Time Magazine* ('The Longest Run', 1 August 2016).

Their competing times were not all quite up to Olympic standards, but they competed anyway, many of them runners. Refugees are not animals. They are human beings possessed of the highest dreams and hopes, like any of us. They won the privilege to compete, and they carried an extra impetus. South Sudanese athlete Yiech Pur Biel is reported to have said: 'I feel a lot of pressure, because millions of refugees are looking for us to tell what they are living, … [and] I want to come back and serve the nation, show them the way as a peacemaker, tell the world we can challenge our leaders' (Price, 'The Longest Run').

In Christianity, we pray for one another and the world, we take on the burdens of others in our hearts, and consequently we shape our lives to ease the troubles of others. Prayer, fasting, working for social justice are examples. Through the experience of running with the memory of these athletes in my heart, it no longer mattered what my time might be. It only mattered that we were treading a landscape of dusty, interminable effort, pushing towards new ideas about what any of us can do, and towards the real beauty of being a human. For me, the goal of peace and justice was beyond the finishing line, a larger political and spiritual reality, nourished by the contest and the effort it cost.

It was finally race day. I felt a bit strung out sitting in the car. I'd been up since 4.00 a.m. When I got up I ate a bagel, drank coffee, tried to act normally – but my stomach was doing flipflops. I took two pre-emptive ibuprofen tablets, hoping to minimize any pain I might feel. My sister drove me from Santa Cruz to Half Moon Bay. We left home in the dark, and we arrived at the starting point still in the dark. What the hell was I doing? I wondered.

At the very time we were driving to Half Moon Bay, the country was waking up to news of a blast that had rocked the Chelsea neighbourhood of Manhattan the night before, and a frightening story about eight people who were injured in a mass stabbing in a mall in Minnesota. The war in Syria was ramping up. US airstrikes were dropping bombs on Syrian forces. The media showed chilling photos of crumbled concrete buildings, bloodied bodies. It was reported that militants had killed 17 soldiers at an Indian army base in Kashmir. Earlier that day, 18 September, at a Fun Run in New Jersey, a pipe bomb exploded – though with no casualties, thank God.

Dangers and threats to life were everywhere. I hadn't heard about the pipe bomb in New Jersey before I crossed the starting line. Later, it was scary to realize innocuous events like community runs had become terrorist targets. But even if I'd known, I'd still have run. Perhaps the best I could do was to join in a group of people testing their strength and endurance playfully. Games are part of the beauty of human civilization – like dance, liturgy, art in every form, and the pursuit of knowledge. If we are going to claim the high ground, we need to have the courage to be the kind of people we want to be all the time.

As we drove along Highway 1, emergency vehicles passed us. Lots of them. It turned out that the General Store in Pescadero had burned down. But not knowing this, the pre-race drive had an aura of crisis – a real-life emergency. Yet I'd paid $170 to run this marathon; nothing would stop me now.

Because it was dark there was no view visible as we drove this famously exquisite route between Santa Cruz and Half Moon Bay. We sat in the car. My sister drove. We listened to PIG radio. 'What's that?' I asked. She told me, and I immediately forgot. The jitters were taking over my mind and body. I knew I should never have signed up for this marathon. I'd done it in a flash of wishful thinking – under the impression that a marathon would prove that I was a real runner. Incredible naivete. Another ageing macho man out to prove himself to himself, and the world that doesn't care, the accusing voices chorused in my head.

I took long shuddering breaths. I tried to give myself solace, to sweet talk myself: 'You'll do fine', 'It's not winning that counts', 'Suit up, show up, have a good time'. What a colossal load of platitudinous crap! I thought.

'What if I can't finish?' I asked my sister.

'It'll be a great story!' she said, taking another slug of her kale, berry and banana smoothie.

'Right,' I muttered. I shoved my hands into my crotch to stop them from shaking. I knew my teeth would start chattering if I relaxed the tiniest bit.

'Breathe!' I told myself. I drew long shuddering breaths. I applied myself to living in the moment, closely examining the dashboard of the car. I rubbed my hand across the upholstery of the car seat. I tried to listen to the man singing on the radio. It sounded like Country and Western. What is PIG radio? (WPIG is the local radio station.) My sister has always been ten steps ahead of me, cool-factor-wise. She drinks smoothies for breakfast, listens to PIG radio. I wished I'd eaten a steak, but the email from the race organizers said to eat lightly before the race. I even got the idea it might be better not to eat for 15 hours before the race, so my gastrointestinal tract would be clear. I began to worry about the breakfast I ate; I feared I'd shit myself and become a pariah on the trail!

I'd smeared Vaseline on my feet, crotch, armpits, nipples. No friction – I didn't want any bleeding sores. I'd never had that happen on one of my training runs, but I was convinced it would happen to me on this marathon. Just the name 'marathon' astounded me. I am not the sort of person who runs marathons. I lounge in coffee shops, I read books until my eyes burn. What on earth am I doing? I felt like a greased pig. God grant me the serenity to accept the things I cannot change. I asked myself: what exactly can I not change at this moment? I only need to say the word and it's off. This is all my fault and I can fix it with a graceful admission that I'd made a mistake. It was a textbook example of all-or-nothing alcoholic thinking: running a marathon as my first race! I'm 58. I don't need to prove anything to anybody.

On second thoughts, I needed to simply accept that I'd developed a bad case of pre-race anxiety. It was what it was. God helping me, I'd be able to move beyond these feelings, but they were the real deal now ... The courage to change the things I can: I've had jitters before and worked through them.

'Remember when I was in the Great American Think-Off?' I asked my sister. 'I was pretty scared before that, too.'

She reached over and patted my knee. 'Yep - and you won' (O'Mara, 'Honest to Goodness Priest...' *Baltimore Sun*, 23 June 1998).

The GPS suddenly indicated a sharp left turn ahead. We were in Half Moon Bay, approaching the starting point. Cars and people flashed in our headlights. It was 6.00 a.m. In an hour, I'd be running. We nosed around blindly, then pulled up next to another car that had people in running clothes next to it. 'This must be it,' I said weakly.

An extremely handsome man with bulging quads and biceps in filmy running gear spoke to us. He had what sounded like a French accent. An international runner. Who did I think I was to sign up for an event like this? We followed him to the sign-in table, near where they were setting up the marquees for the concessions, and the techies were erecting the starting/finishing line with its electronic clock to track our times to the second. I'd checked in weeks ago at a running store in San Francisco, but it seemed like a good thing to double-check. I joined the queue of Latino men, South Asians, Europeans, lean and strong as pumas. Lithe women with pony tails and sun visors bounced around nonchalantly. I was number 20.

My sister and I walked around. She was trying to take my mind off my troubles. 'Isn't that darling?' she pointed to a house. We looked at a wedding venue with an arch decorated in last night's blossoms. 'This is wonderful!' she exclaimed. I grunted.

Half an hour to go. I got my photo taken by an excessively upbeat man; the bay was behind me. The early dawn light gleamed from a rip in the seam of the horizon. The sun was chafing like a champion to run its course. More people arrived. A senior-looking woman with feathers in her hair. Large-sized people. Men and women at least 20 years older than I was. I knew who I'd be running with. At least I wouldn't be all alone the whole way.

At 6.55 a.m. the announcer came on the air, directing us to line up: elite runners to the front, 'bucket-listers' to the back– so we wouldn't get trampled on. He introduced an Olympic gold medallist who would be running the course. Much later, I think I got a glimpse of him. As I was approaching my halfway mark, he was thundering past me on the home stretch.

Full marathon runners would leave at 7.00 a.m., half marathon runners would leave at 7.15 a.m. I wished I'd had the humility and presence of mind to sign up for the half marathon. I heard that a bus would be deployed at 1.00 p.m. to pick up everyone still on the course. I prayed, 'Please God, don't let the bus get me!'

A man in a power-black running outfit, obviously just arrived, asked me: 'What's going on?' Looking him up and down, I pointed to the front: 'Elite runners go up front. Me, I'm in the back!' Grinning, he slapped me on the shoulder. 'I'm with you!'

I looked at my fellow runners. Some were laughing and talking, but most were looking pensive, concentrating, and conserving their energy. My stomach got tighter and tighter. Finally, it was 'ten, nine, eight, seven, six ...' and we were off.

I heard my sister shouting 'Go, Clark!' I ran towards her to smile and wave. Only God knew what was in store, but no more second-guessing myself. I had only one thing to do: run. I gently picked my way around some people in front of me, looked for openings in the crowd. I could feel my legs responding like they have always responded, the muscles moving, my feet tap-tap-tapping on the pavement. Some people waved and shouted, 'Good luck!' One woman said, 'You're crazy!' I kept up with the guy in black. We got in behind two women who were having a lively conversation. It felt easy, normal, and unextraordinary.

The route threaded through some commercial warehouses, then took a sweeping turn uphill towards what looked like an enormous golf ball on a tee. Some kind of reactor? Surely not in Half Moon Bay, California. A laboratory, maybe?

We scrambled over a gate and left the pavement. It was uphill. The gravel path steepened; it got warmer. Some people were slowing down, pulling to the side. I realized with joy I could pull ahead of some of them.

Hoodies and T-shirts began to appear on the ground; people were dropping layers of clothing. I'd read about this practice. I would hate to throw a sweatshirt to the ground, never to see it again. Plus, I'd taken the pre-race advice to alter nothing from our training procedures and was wearing only what I always wore: hat, T-shirt, shorts, ankle socks and shoes. Start shedding anything and I'd be naked quite quickly.

The smell was wonderful – the dry tang of grass and shrubs. The air sharp and salty. As the sun came up it burned the fog off the bay, and I could see the sea below. I could give myself to this: a billion-dollar view. My legs felt strong, I was breathing easily. I remembered I like to run.

Since it was Sunday morning, I began to recite Mass in my head. 'Glory to God in the highest …' I intoned to myself. We trotted over hills, up and down, until finally we emerged on pavement again, a steep hill.

Finally, at what seemed the back edge of a parking lot, we rounded a bright orange cone. It must have been the four- or five-mile mark. I felt completely alive. I could think of nothing else I wanted to do or anywhere else I wanted to be. People were smiling and waving as I passed them – I was in the middle of the pack, ahead of the guy in the black power suit and the lady with feathers.

Boy Scouts, church groups and runner support groups were stationed all along the route handing out Gu – something like what I imagine astronaut food to be like, nasty and nutritious – and water and 'electrolytes'. It wasn't Gatorade, it didn't have any taste at all. But I always took some when I needed a drink, though at this stage I wasn't drinking at every station. Everyone was upbeat. The whole experience was elating.

We wound back off the mountain, past the white reactor thing. The pack began to stretch out as we went down the long incline. Some seemed to really let go. I tried to hold back. My experience during training had been that running downhill could up the ante on my pace and I'd be flailing along too fast too soon, quickly exhausted. Then we were back to the starting point, mile 8 or 9. There was my sister shouting encouragement, waving her coffee cup, shooting a home video on her phone: 'Go, Sweetie!' she called out. I was feeling giddy. I could feel the months of training paying off. My breath was regular. I was warm, my legs and arms were moving smoothly, and my neck was supple.

'Run and feel the Lord's pleasure!' Indeed, it felt very good to run, my chosen sport. We headed south out of town along the waterfront. The beach was to my right – beautiful homes and parks were on the left. It was flat, smooth, salty fresh.

At about mile 14 I began to feel some pressure in my bowels, but fortunately there was a toilet there and I suffered no indignities – though, as I emerged, I saw people I'd passed now ahead of me. This was about the length of a normal training run. I'd trained half a dozen times on a route in San Francisco from our friary on Dolores Street across from the Dolores Park to the Cliff House restaurant out on the ocean beach, running through Golden Gate Park. A couple of times I'd doubled up on portions of it, meaning I ran 22 miles, and these had been extremely hard runs.

At mile 16 on this, my first marathon, I turned to follow the course away from the shore towards a beach community. The race route was in and around a group of suburban houses.

Suddenly I didn't see anybody. Had I taken a wrong turn? No, there were signs on traffic cones. It seemed much warmer among the houses. My breath was getting ragged, my feet, legs, back and shoulders were twinging from time to time. But I'd expected this, so I slowed the pace a bit to conserve my strength, and kept going.

Was it possible I still had 10 miles to go? I focused on my breath. I began to recite my running mantras: 'This is the way Franciscans run, Franciscans run, Franciscans run, this is the way Franciscans run so early in the morning.' I sang it to a tune my father used to sing while bouncing us on his knee: 'This is the way the farmer rides, the farmer rides, the farmer rides, this is the way the farmer rides so early in the morning.'

I trotted along trying not to think 'Ten more miles, my God!' Now as I approached water stations I came to a complete halt to drink, breathe. Standing still for 20 seconds was a great relief to my legs. Mile 16, 17. 'You're doing great, 20! Keep going!' a man shouted out to me, using the number pinned to my shirt. I gave him a thumbs-up.

I started to become aware of inspirational quotes posted along the route. Were there similar signs at the start of the race? I couldn't remember. These exhorted us not to give up, to be courageous, to acknowledge the joy and significance of running.

I needed every encouraging word, like this one: 'We run to undo the damage we've done to body and spirit. We run to find some part of ourselves yet undiscovered' (John 'The Penguin' Bingham).

Everything was getting worse. I ran across a field, through a forest. By now my calves hurt, my feet felt swollen, my back and shoulders were extremely painful. I couldn't find any comfortable way to hold myself. I was completely wet with perspiration, and could feel it sheeting down my chest, my back. Sweat streamed down my inner thighs.

'Drink water!' I told myself. 'Don't stop!' I plodded on. Runners passed me going in both directions. Most had looks of complete concentration on their faces,but they would still acknowledge me. Some said 'Good work! Keep it up!' I always reciprocated: 'Yeah, you too!' I began to suspect, though, that the course designers had messed up the mile markers. The distance between them seemed much greater than before. Finally, I staggered on to the Ritz-Carlton golf course. I passed a woman who was saying to her companion: 'In New York they would never have a race right through the hotel!'

I could see my fellow runners, strung out around the path going around the hotel. On the hotel terrace, people sipped lattes, read the paper. Some seemed to be trying to ignore the marathoners; others smiled at us.

There was a particularly steep hill, with a photographer at the top: 'Smile for me!' he said. I managed a grin and a thumbs-up. Still going. Then down the other side, a precipitous drop, mile 19. Then turn around: right back up that damn hill. I slowed to a walk. 'Finish the distance!' I said to myself. I looked at my watch – just after 11.00 a.m. I could easily run 7 miles in an hour. But I had no idea what those 7 miles might be like.

Just after cresting the hill after the turn- around, I began to run again downhill, circling the hotel terrace. It was then I felt, for the first time, terrible cramps in my legs. It was as if grappling hooks were buried in my thighs. I cried out. The pain in my shoulders and back were nothing compared to this. Plus, my feet felt like raw meat, bruised, soft and pulpy, though when I finally took off my shoes at the end of the race, my feet looked fine. Stopping to assuage the cramps, my vision clouded.

I had queasy memories of the time I'd passed out in July after a long training run in Milne Bay Province, Papua New Guinea. On that occasion, I'd done about 9 miles in 85 degrees Fahrenheit. As I'd straightened up after bending to fill my water bottle from the water tank, I felt my vision cloud over. My arms were exceedingly heavy. I had no power to catch myself. I heard myself give a plaintive 'Ooof!' sound, like you hear when you accidentally step on a frog at night on the road in the Solomon Islands.

Then the next thing I knew, I was on my back, in the muddy grass, with three brothers staring down at me with sheer panic on their faces: 'Brother! Brother! Are you okay?'

'Well, no,' I said, 'but I will get better. It's just the heat, dehydration and exhaustion. Otherwise I feel fine,' I said, trying to reassure them.

That was then; this was now – 5 miles to go. I knew with grim understanding I was a nanosecond away from passing out again.

My vision cleared when I moved. It was standing still and bending over that was the bad part. Walking was okay, but I'd signed up for a marathon, damn it, so I was going to run. Walk, run 100 paces. Stop. Bend to catch my breath. Feel woozy. Clutch at a post, pole, tree or bench.

'Careful, Clark.' Careful, careful, careful. Eventually, I noticed two other men doing the same run/walk, stop/go. As they came up to me, one said: 'Cramps?'

'Ah-yayaya,' I said.

'Same here. Him too, I think,' he said, pointing at the other man. 'Good luck!'

We wasted no more breath in conversation. Soon it was 12.15 p.m. I had about two and a half miles to go.

I changed my running mantra: 'One more step!' I told myself. 'One more step.' These were the words a friend who is now very elderly – nearly 95 – gave me when I asked his advice about running a marathon. 'Just tell yourself, "One more step!" and that's how you finish a marathon. I've run lots of marathons, haven't I, dear?' he asked his wife. 'Yes,' she replied, starting to tick off: 'New York, Boston …'

Suddenly, my sister was there with my niece's dog, Paka, on a lead. 'Clark! Oh, my God! Drink water! Sit down! Are you okay?'

'I'm fine, I've been drinking water. I am NOT going to sit down. But it is really good to see you! How far?'

'About 2 miles. Drink your water! You aren't drinking enough! Sit down! You remind me of Dad,' she said. Our father had died 15 months earlier.

'Do you mean in his doggedness? Yep, that's me.'

We pressed on, making querulous conversation. First, I'd run ahead, then walking she would catch up as I stopped to gather myself. Then a purple woman stopped me – a purple outfit, purple hair – or was I now imagining things?

'Are you okay?' she asked.

'No,' I gasped. My sister couldn't hear me, I'd got ahead of her.

'Cramps? Dizzy?' she asked.

'Yes. I'm 58 years old, this is my first marathon. I don't think I can do it.'

'Sure, you can, honey. Here, sit down. Open your mouth. This is salt. Then drink this warm water. This will take care of your cramps. Now drink these electrolytes, which will help with the dizziness. Okay. You can make it, it's just around those grey buildings you see there. Go!' What an angel!

I ran with new determination. Soon, my niece was there. 'Go, Clark, you're almost done!' My brother-in-law: 'My God, Clark, you've almost done it, keep going. About half a mile more!'

I blundered on. Back through the warehouses we'd so blithely run past earlier. A worker in a fluorescent vest waved me around a corner: 'Your last corner. Two blocks!'

Then, I could see the finishing line; I could hear people shouting.

Then, I couldn't hear anything. I was stationary, bent over. 'O my God, O my God,' I said to myself. 'No, no, no.'

Another woman came over to me. 'Are you okay?'

'No!' I shouted. 'I can't do it.'

'Yes, you can!' she yelled back, and pulled my arm. 'Run,' she screamed. 'Go on!'

So, drawing a deep breath and holding it, I gathered my strength, stretched my head forward, and ran for that finishing line. Five hours, fifty-eight minutes and two seconds – less than two minutes to go before they pulled the plug on the event. I was the last person to get an official time.

All was confusion: people shouting, hugging, snapping photos. There was a roar in my ears.

I was embraced by my sister and her family. I felt as if I'd barely survived the ordeal. Later I'd see photos of the awards ceremony they'd held hours earlier: the cheques awarded to the winners, the speeches, the radiant, happy faces of the runners who'd already finished. That's what the world loves to see: the image of well-trained, happy athletes celebrating. Looking around, the area was practically deserted. They'd all gone home. There were heaps of bananas and bottled water unattended. The event was over. Shuddering, gagging, barely able to stand, I only wanted to weep.

A new story was emerging, scrawled across my life. Finisher. I'd done the only thing I had to do. The early elation and the concluding agony were both true, both integral parts of the experience. I have a list of many things I'd do differently – *will* do differently, next time. Yet among the marquees of the empty space of that finishing line, a spirit of something new fluttered the canvas flaps. Peace. Inner peace. I never had to run the race. The sort of insight that only comes with hindsight. I have plenty of credentials as a runner just going out day after day. But I'd overcome a lot of fear to do this.

There is another kind of victory – not of winning a race but of having simply participated in one. It's like being a friar. Rational calculations would have dissuaded me from testing my vocation: it's not the way to power and prominence, and flies in the face of every culture's notions of personal fulfilment and a happy family life.

Thank God, I took a chance on it, or I'd never have known the fulfilment and happiness I have in my life. This is the victory of faith. Christ came not to take away our struggle but to be with us in it. At every step of the way, I have never been alone in my vocation – least of all, on this ball-buster of a marathon. The path of testing and discovery was always going to lead to this deeper understanding.

Even if I had been scooped up by the bus at 1.00 p.m., it would have been, as my sister said, a good story.

Afterword

Running to resurrection means reaching out for what Eugene Peterson calls 'robust maturity', accepting a sober assessment of my life's progress and the choices I've made with the gifts and qualities with which I've been endowed. Maturity does not mean settling for something less than I'd hoped for – a middle-aged compromise. Rather, growing up seems to mean going deeper into the joys and satisfactions that are available to me, the comforts of familiar habits, and the thrill of radical choices in new directions. Fulfilling my obligation to serve my brothers and others in my travels around the world was, overall, a great joy.

I'm glad it wasn't a lifetime appointment, however. The running routes I've forged have served several functions: to be fully present in the particular place and circumstances. They have helped me to see, smell and experience life in many contexts down on the pavement, unprotected from people, vehicles and weather. Also, my running routes continue to serve as meditative journeys, recollecting and integrating who I am as a man, an evangelist and friar, sharing the truth about Christ as I discover him in day-to-day life.

As a young man, I tried to finesse some of my own concerns and challenges: glossing over some, and shying away from and denying those too painful to face. Consequently, for much of my life I have been unable to understand the larger implications of resurrection. God raised Jesus from the dead to make all things new, except me, I felt. But now I have come to know that the vicissitudes of life in its various challenges show even more beautifully the breadth and depth of Christian teaching about God's commitment to the whole created order. To share my experience of God in all the beauty I have seen requires that I tell the many ways God has come to me in my sexual identity, in recovery from compulsive drinking, in my Franciscan vocation, in a physical turn-around and embrace of a sport that has provided a metaphor or container for the body of my experiences.

I have written this book to demonstrate that being physically active, as much as we are able, is an important part of the spiritual life. Our bodies are not to be ignored, but loved, cherished, trusted and disciplined, so that we can live vigorously, more joyfully. While the body doesn't perform the same every day – it's not a machine – determination, repetition-training and effort can become a frame of reference for more in life than just sport. There are no guarantees about happiness, but paying attention to a bodily felt way of knowing can help unravel the Gordian knots with which overthinking too often snarls our lives.

Another reason I have written this book is to tell my story about vocation. Inside religious life there are gifts. Finding a God-created home among others in a faith community is a big gift. Part of this giftedness in the twenty-first century is honouring our sexuality and our bodies in a frank and matter-of-fact way: integration of sexuality is essential to maturity.

And it is a spiritual matter. There is not one simple way of being a 'sexual celibate' (see Goergen, *The Sexual Celibate*), and the catalogue of factors that go into the cost and promise of every decision to test such a vocation is huge. But sexuality serves our vocation. My sexual identity has made me the friar I am. I have had a gay person's sense of differentness from early in life. Drinkers often confess to feeling different too. I have developed compassion, and that comes from growing up with same-sex attraction in a hostile world and understanding the predicament of other outcasts. Thank God, there are significant changes in attitudes towards homosexuality in some places.

These qualities of compassion and understanding facilitate embracing a religious vocation – a Franciscan calling to poverty, chastity and obedience, and care for the poor, and for marginalized outcasts – that goes against the cultural norms and expectations of every culture I've ever encountered. Sensitivity to beauty – a gay marker for sure – is part of that vocation, but who could miss the love of beauty in 'The Canticle of the Creatures'? And now, when the desire for physical contact grips me, I can run and wake up my body to many other ways of being fully alive.

Perhaps it is no accident that this sense of differentness has led to many attempts to feel less marginalized. Drinking helped me, but then betrayed me. Free now of a desire to drink, I know too the consolation that the truth will set you free, regardless of how tentatively I approached that reckoning. Thus, I have a pastoral ministry of spiritual friendship in which I share that discovery of freedom. I also have a political commitment to speak the truth about myself as a gay man and a friar.

Becoming physically active has been key for pulling everything together in my life. Feeling better and stronger physically has strengthened my self-confidence and encouraged me to share my story. As a result, what I think and what I do are coming closer together. I am only an occasional hypocrite now. In moments of stress, the lag time between reaction and response is getting shorter and shorter – from a decade in the case of a long-held resentment, to just a few hours on normal days, perhaps just minutes on my best days.

I don't suppose I'll ever eradicate that first shock of anger or fear or hate or whatever emotional reaction I might have. But with attentiveness and practice, in time I find I can respond honestly, charitably and more helpfully. And there is no fault in pausing to breathe and consider, even if you are running a marathon. I used to think the rash reaction was the unvarnished truth; but now I view it as no less conditioned a response than patience, fortitude and generosity.

American culture rewards brash and aggressive behaviour. As I have got stronger with exercise, my body has 'naturally' adjusted to greater and greater challenges. What was once impossible is now achievable and, in many ways, considered normal activity. So too with my mind – as I have practised honesty, patience and courage I can now 'intuitively handle those situations that used to baffle' me, as we say in recovery. The times when I 'lose it' are fewer and, when I do unravel emotionally, I continue to learn better how to get the help I need.

Becoming more aware of myself has been challenged by travel. The distractions of different places can take me out of myself. At the same time, the travel has abetted my efforts to 'practise resurrection' because in each new situation, in each new culture, and relationship, I am asking myself, 'Who am I?' I take time to think about what is essential and what is not, what are the non-negotiables. I can basically eat anything, sleep on any surface, manage muddy trails, ford rivers, and ride out storms at sea. I can sit on cramped aeroplanes: it's all adventure.

I am blessed with an Anglican Franciscan culture that exists around the world. We use the same office book for prayers, the Eucharistic liturgies are very much the same, and the habits, the Rule and the documents governing our life in the most important ways are the same the world over. The essential tests have been responding generously when I am tired, finding ways of dealing with difficulties, and getting the guidance and sustenance I need to stay spiritually fit.

Support groups have been few and far between. My confessor lives in New Jersey. I've had to be vulnerable enough in conversation with brothers to get the emotional support I crave without compromising anybody, and at the same time negotiating a sometimes-tricky path between very different cultures. It's when I want somebody to look me in the eye and tell me exactly what they are thinking that I am most American and least effective, and hence most easily frustrated.

Running has shaped my soul as much as it has strengthened my body. My spirituality is deeply characterized by all that I experience while running. My soul needs time for quiet reflection and I need time to sweat. I need to set goals for myself and push myself to meet them. Spiritual survival depends on humbly accepting that some things are beyond my control. I am not a superman. I follow Jesus who was born in a stable, who died on the cross. His teachings were mostly parables. My hope is that these stories might agitate and inspire, subvert your fears, and embolden your desire to thrive and to make the world a better place too.

There were several congratulatory texts and phone calls after the Half Moon Bay Marathon. There had been prayers offered up on my behalf throughout the race, and good wishes tendered. When I got back to the friary in San Francisco, the front door was crowded with congratulatory balloons – There were even flowers in my room. That evening we had a big chocolate cake and they gave me a card. One brother gave me a dollar per mile out of his fortnightly allowance of $50; I immediately put it into a church collection plate, returned to continue God's work. No way could I use that money for myself. It took weeks for my body to fully recover, but long term my reaction was more emotional than physical. I understand postpartum blues a bit more sympathetically, though I'll never know for sure.

A month after the race I was at a dinner party in Australia talking with a man who had coached runners. As he listened to my story of the marathon and my near collapse, he laughed with recognition. He explained a little bit about diet, oxygen in the blood, different training strategies, and the mental toughness that is required as much as the physical strength. This was good news! I could understand his comments with greater insight. I wanted to apply them to my running practice. As we were called to table, I began to imagine the next time, another run. During dinner our host said, 'What have you learned tonight?'

'I'm an athlete,' I said, adding to the words that suggest who

I am, who I might become. I am a Christian. I am a grateful, recovering alcoholic. I am gay. I am a celibate friar. I am a cook, brother, son, friend, writer, teacher, preacher, priest, adventurous reader, spiritual 'warrior', traveller and pilgrim.

A running friar, sharing cramps with marathoners over thousands of years, I am also heir to a spiritual tradition and vocation of one of the greatest athletes of God the world has ever known. Christian history is full of difficult things, and the Franciscans have had their share in that difficult history. But there has been an enduring Promethean message of hope that has contributed to the liberation of humanity, demonstrated in the spiritual fire let loose in the world in St Francis of Assisi. The brightness of his example shines in the world, illuminating dark corners and work to be done. The key is not to forget our pasts but to draw strength from our experiences. Then we are able to serve the world with generosity and gratitude. As Wendell Berry says in his poem, 'No, No, There Is No Going Back':

> No, no, there is no going back.
> Less and less you are
> that possibility you were.
> More and more you have become
> those lives and deaths
> that have belonged to you.
> You have become a sort of grave
> containing much that was
> and is no more in time, beloved
> then, now, and always.
> And so you have become a sort of tree
> standing over the grave.
> Now more than ever you can be
> generous toward each day
> that comes, young, to disappear
> forever, and yet remain

unaging in the mind.
Every day you have less reason
not to give yourself away.

(Berry, 'No, No, There Is No Going Back', *This Day*, p. 141)

References and Further Reading

Online

Berry, Wendell, *The Sabbath Poems*. Available at: http://inwardoutward.org/the-church-of-the-saviour/churches.

Buckley, Michael J., 'The Wisdom of Rev. Michael J. Buckley, S.J.: The Downward Path', *Servant-Leader Associates*. Available at:www.servant-leaderassociates.com/Servant-Leader_Associates/ Faith_Perspectives_files/The%20Wisdom%20of%20Rev%20 Michael%20J%20Buckley.pdf (accesssed 22.11.16). The document states: 'Father Buckley addressed a community of priests in training on the occasion of the completion of their work at the Jesuit School of Theology at Berkeley. He posed a very fundamental question and yet one at variance to the conventional wisdom of our day. He asked his young colleagues, not if they were strong enough for their vocation, but if they were weak enough.'

Carr Rowland, E., *Faithful Unto Death: The Story of the New Guinea Martyrs* (Stanmore, NSW.: Australian Board of Missions, 1964). Available at: http://anglicanhistory.org/aus/png/rowland_ faithful1964.html (Accessed 13.4.19)

'Franciscans and the Holy Land: Interview with Vicar of Custody, 13th March 2005', *Zenit*. Available at: https://zenit. org/articles/franciscans-and-the-holy-land/ (accessed 8.12.18).

McClung, John, 'Runners You Should Know: The Hopi', *Barefoot in Arizona* (a blog). Available at: http://bfinaz.blogspot.com/2012/09/ runners-you-should-know-hopi.html (accessed 26.11.16).

Oliver, Steven, 'Hate He Said'. Available at :http://anitaheissblog.

blogspot.co.uk/2012/05/steven-oliver-hate-he-said.html (Accessed 9.12.16).

Oliver, Steven, 'Me I Am', Available at: http://anitaheissblog. blogspot.com/2012/05/steven-oliver-me-i-am.html (Accessed 23.11.16). Steven performed this piece at the Kuril Dhagun Indigenous Knowledge Centre at the State Library of Queensland as part of the 'Am I Black Enough For You?' event on 1 May 2012.

Sammis, John H., – 'Trust and Obey', 1887. Available at: www.godtube.com>popular-hymns>trust-and-obey.

Southern Poverty Law Center, 'Climate of Fear: Latino Immigrants in Suffolk County, NY', Available at: www.splcenter. org/20090831/climate-fear-latino-immigrants-suffolk-county-ny (accessed 13.4.19).

'Unitatis Redintegratio: Second Vatican Council Decree on Ecumenism', 21 November 1964. Available at: www.vatican. va/archive/hist_councils/ii_vatican_council/documents/vat-ii_decree_19641121_unitatis-redintegratio_en.html (accessed 10.4.19).

'Whenever I feel the Urge to Exercise I Lie Down Until It Goes Away', *Quote Investigator.* Available at: http://quoteinvestigator. com/2012/06/09/urge-to-exercise (accessed 9.12.16).

Yad Vashem (2019). *Yad Vashem. The World Holocaust Remembrance Center.* Available at: www.yadvashem.org (accessed 11.4.19).

Publications

Angier, Natalie, 'No Time for Bullies: Baboons Retool their Culture', *New York Times*, 13 April 2004.

Armstrong, Kristin, 'Why I Run', *Runner's World*, 18 October 2006. Available at: www.runnersworld.com/women/a20800675/why-i-run (accessed 15.6.19).

Armstrong, Regis, *Clare of Assisi: The Lady* (New Hyde Park, NY: New City Press, 2006).

Armstrong, Regis J., J. A. Wayne Hellmann, William J. Short, eds, *Francis of Assisi: Early Documents*, vol. 1, The Saint (New

York: New City Press, 1999).

Armstrong, Regis J., J. A. Wayne Hellmann, William J. Short, eds, *Francis of Assisi: Early Documents*, vol. 2, The Founder (New York: New City Press, 2000).

Armstrong, Regis J., J. A. Wayne Hellmann, William J. Short, eds, *Francis of Assisi: Early Documents*, vol. 3, The Prophet (New York: New City Press, 2001).

Augustine, *Confessions I.1*, trans. Henry Chadwick (Oxford: Oxford University Press, 2008).

Beauvois, Xavier, *Of Gods and Men* (Why Not Productions, 2010).

Becker, Ann M., *Images of America: Mount Sinai* (Charleston, SC: Arcadia, 2003).

Benton, Nicholas F., *Extraordinary Hearts: Reclaiming Gay Sensibility's Central Role in the Progress of Civilization* (Maple Shade, NJ: Lethe Press, 2013).

Berry, Wendell, *New Collected Poems* (Berkeley, CA: Counterpoint, 2013).

Berry, Wendell, *This Day: Collected and New Sabbath Poems* (Berkeley, CA: Counterpoint, 2014).

The Book of Common Prayer 1979 (New York: Church Publishing, 2014).

Brother Sun, Sister Moon (1972). Franco Zeffirelli. Euro International Film (EIA).

Cardinal Hugolini of Conti of Segni, 'Memoriale Propositi', 16, in G. G. Meersseman OP, *Dossier de L'Ordre de la Pénitence: au XIIIe Siècle* (Fribourg: Editions Universitaires Fribourg Suisse, 1961).

Chariots of Fire (1981). Hugh Hudson. UK: Twentieth Century Fox, Allied Stars Ltd, Enigma Productions.

The Daily Office SSF, revd edn (London: Mowbray, 2010).

Dunstan, Petà, *This Poor Sort: A History of the European Province of the Society of St Francis* (London: Darton, Longman and Todd, 1997).

Fox, Matthew, *Sins of the Spirit, Blessings of the Flesh: Transforming*

Evil in Soul and Society, revd edn (Berkeley, CA: North Atlantic Books, 2016).

Gendlin, Eugene T., *Focusing* (New York: Dodd, Mead & Co., 1978).

Goergen, Donald, *The Sexual Celibate* (New York: Seabury Press, 1975).

Gooder, Paula, *Body: Biblical Spirituality for the Whole Person* (London: SPCK, 2016).

Hardy, Thomas, *Tess of the d'Urbervilles: A Pure Woman Faithfully Presented* (New York: Harper and Brothers, 1892).

Hillman, James, *Loose Ends* (Washington, DC: Spring Publications, 1975).

Homer, *The Odyssey of Homer*, trans. Richard Lattimore (New York: HarperCollins, 2007).

Institute for BioSpiritual Research, 'Why Biospiritual Focusing?' *The BioSpiritual Institute, Inc..* Available at:biospiritual.org/why-biospiritual-focusing/(accessed 5.12.16).

Julien FMIC, Danielle, 'Clare's Model of Leadership', *The Cord*, 51.4 (2001), 184.

Kramer, Jane, 'The Philosopher Chef', *The New Yorker*, 3 December 2012.

Lee, Rhodi, 'Infanticide: Biggest Threat to Baby Chacma Baboons? Adult Males (and here's what females do to prevent it)', *Tech Times*, 14 November 2014.

Matthews, W. H., *Mazes and Labyrinths: Their History and Development* (London: Dover, 2011).

Maurin, Peter, *Easy Essays* (Chicago: Franciscan Herald Press, 1984).

McCormack OSF, Dorothy, 'The Essential Elements of the Evangelical Life of Franciscans', *The Cord*, 38.8 (1988), 243.

McKibben, Bill, *The Age of Missing Information* (New York: Plume, 1993).

Nhat Hanh, Thich, *Peace is Every Step: The Path of Mindfulness in Everyday Life* (New York: Bantam, 1992).

Nouwen, Henri, *The Genesee Diary: Report from a Trappist*

Monastery (New York: Image Books, 1981).

O'Mara, Richard, 'Honest to Goodness Priest tells a Nation Beset with Moral Questioning that Compassion, not Truth, is Always the Best Policy. Amen, Say the Great American Think-Off Judges', *Baltimore Sun*, 23 June 1998. Available at: http://articles. baltimoresun.com/1998-06-23/features/1998174021_1_honesty-mills-regional-cultural-new-york-mills (accessed 9.12.18).

Ottolenghi, Yotam and Sami Tamimi, *Jerusalem* (London: Ebury Press, 2012).

Parry, C. H. H., 'I Was Glad' in Westminster Abbey Choir, *Westminster Abbey Choir* [CD], (London: Hyperion, 2015).

Peterson, Eugene H., *The Message* (Carol Stream, IL: Tyndale House Publishers, 2002).

Peterson, Eugene H., *Practice Resurrection: A Conversation on Growing Up in Christ* (Grand Rapids, MI: Eerdmans, 2010).

Price, S. L., 'The Longest Run', *Time Magazine*, 188.5 (2016), 51.

Richo, David, *The Five Things We Cannot Change: And the Happiness We Find By Embracing Them* (Boston, MA: Shambala, 2006).

Richo, David, *When the Past is Present: Healing Emotional Wounds That Sabotage Our Relationships* (Boston, MA: Shambala, 2008).

Richo, David, *Daring to Trust: Opening Ourselves to Real Love and Intimacy* (Boston, MA: Shambala, 2011).

Roth, Gabrielle, *Sweat Your Prayers: The Five Rhythms of the Soul – Movement as Spiritual Practice* (New York: Jeremy P. Tarcher, 1977).

Springsteen, Bruce, *Born to Run* (New York: Simon and Schuster, 2016).

Teilhard de Chardin, Pierre, *Hymn of the Universe* (New York: Harper and Row, 1961).

Thomas, Elizabeth Marshall, *The Hidden Life of Dogs* (New York: Houghton Mifflin Company, 1993).

Traherne, Thomas, *Centuries of Meditations*, ed. Bertram Dobell

(London: P. J. and A. E. Dobell, 1934).

Veriditas. Available at: www.veriditas.org/ (accessed 11.4.19)

Williams, Rowan, *Silence and Honey Cakes: The Wisdom of the Desert* (Oxford: Lion Publishing, 2003).

Woodhouse, Patrick, *Etty Hillesum: A Life Transformed* (London: Bloomsbury, 2009).